Study Guide

MW00737333

Cram for the Exam!

Your Guide to Passing the New York Real Estate Salespersons Exam

FOURTH EDITION

Marcia Darvin Spada

CENGAGE
Learning

Australia • Brazil • Japan • Korea • Mexico • Singapore • Spain • United Kingdom • United States

Cram for the Exam! Your Guide to Passing the New York Real Estate Salespersons Exam

Marcia Darvin Spada

Vice President/Editor-in-Chief: Dave Shaut

Executive Editor: Scott Person

Acquisitions Editor: Sara Glassmeyer

Senior Marketing Manager: Mark Linton

Frontlist Buyer, Manufacturing: Kevin Kluck

Art Director: Bethany Casey

Content Project Manager: Jana Lewis

Production Service: PreMedia Global

Cover Image:

Top: Media Bakery, LLC/Purestock

Middle: Media Bakery, LLC/Digital Vision

Bottom: Media Bakery, LLC/Digital Vision

For product information and technology assistance, contact us at **Cengage Learning Customer & Sales Support, 1-800-354-9706**

For permission to use material from this text or product, submit all requests online at **www.cengage.com/permissions** Further permissions questions can be emailed to **permissionrequest@cengage.com**

ISBN-13: 978-0-324-66413-3
ISBN-10: 0-324-66413-3

Cengage Learning
5191 Natorp Boulevard
Mason, OH 45040
USA

Cengage Learning products are represented in Canada by Nelson Education, Ltd.

For your course and learning solutions, visit **academic.cengage.com** Purchase any of our products at your local college store or at our preferred online store **www.ichapters.com**

Printed in the United States of America
1 2 3 4 5 6 7 12 11 10 09 08

Contents

(Continued)

Preface

Congratulations on your decision to invest extra effort to prepare for your qualifying course and state exams. This guide will help you face the exams with greater confidence, which should enhance your test performance.

Cram for the Exam is exactly what it says—a quick way to prepare. Why spend more time than needed? Here you have a directed review in an easy-to-study format. *With Cram for the Exam*, depending on individual needs, you can spend about ten hours for a comprehensive review.

Before you begin your review, take a few minutes to read the first section, *Your Questions Answered*. It gives you details concerning test preparation, time, place, types of questions, and so forth. Also, review the *Quick Tips to Help You Pass*. Then carefully read the instructions on How to Cram for the Exam so you can attain optimum results.

About the Author

Marcia Darvin Spada is owner of the Albany Center for Real Estate Education, a New York–licensed proprietary school. She also is owner of Cram for the Exam, a website that provides practice real estate exams for New York and New Jersey.

A professional educator and nationally known real estate author, Marcia teaches real estate and has developed curricula and many other materials for numerous real estate courses. Her books, courses, and other materials are widely used by colleges, real estate-related organizations, and proprietary schools throughout the country. In addition to *Cram for Exam: Your Guide to Passing the New York Real Estate Salesperson Exam*, she is the author of:

➤ *New York Real Estate for Salespersons*

➤ *New York Real Estate for Brokers*

➤ *Cram for Exam: Your Guide to Passing the New York Real Estate Broker Exam*

➤ *New Jersey Real Estate for Salespersons and Brokers*

➤ *Cram for Exam: Your Guide to Passing the New Jersey Salesperson and Broker Real Estate Exams*

➤ *The Home Inspection Book: A Guide for Professionals*

➤ *Environmental Issues and the Real Estate Professional*

Marcia holds a BA and an MA in English from the State University of New York at Albany and a BS in Real Estate Studies from Empire State College. She welcomes all comments and questions about the material in this textbook. Her website http://www.cramforexam.net contains downloadable practice real estate NYS licensing exams and licensure information. Her e-mail address is cramforexam@hotmail.com.

Acknowledgments

Sincere appreciation goes to my husband, Eugene R. Spada, Esq., for his ongoing help and support in the writing of this exam guide. I am also very grateful to my editorial assistant, Hannah Nightingale, who worked very hard to help me prepare the manuscript.

A very sincere note of gratitude to Acquisitions Editor Sara Glassmeyer of Cengage Learning whose encouragement and assistance has been invaluable in completing all of the New York textbooks. I also appreciate the assistance of Senior Marketing Director Mark Linton, Executive Editor Scott Person, and Real Estate National Account Managers Sheila Cole, and Michelle Kavanaugh, all of Cengage Learning.

Your Questions Answered

1. How do I obtain a salesperson license in New York?

Essentially, you need to complete three steps:
- ✓ Complete a New York State–approved 75-hour qualifying course including the course exam
- ✓ Pass the New York State licensure exam
- ✓ Obtain broker sponsorship

2. What exams must I pass to obtain salesperson licensure in New York?

All applicants for a New York salesperson license must pass the exam given in class at the completion of the 75-hour course. Applicants must also pass an exam given by the Department of State (DOS), the New York regulatory agency that oversees the licensure process.

3. When and where are these exams given?

The 75-hour qualifying course exam generally is given in the classroom at the completion of the 75-hour course by the entity offering the course. The New York State exam is given at DOS test centers throughout the state. See Figure I.1 for a list of exam locations. To verify these locations, check this list on the DOS website.
Web Info: http://www.dos.state.ny.us.

4. Do I need to schedule an appointment to take the NYS licensure exam?

Applicants are required to schedule their real estate salesperson exam on the new DOS Occupational Licensing Management System, e*AccessNY*. In addition to being able to apply for the exam on e*AccessNY*, applicants can view their scheduled exam details or exam results and apply for their salesperson license online. The system provides for access with a personal ID and password that applicants create when they register online. Persons with disabilities who require accessibility information should call 518-473-2731. Applicants who require testing modifications should not schedule an exam and should instead call 518-473-2731.

5. When do I receive my exam results?

Exam results are reported as either passed or failed; applicants will not receive a numerical score. Results are not given over the phone. Exam results are available online by utilizing the account in e*AccessNY*. The exam results are available as soon as possible after the Exam Unit receives the exams and scores them.

6. Should I first complete my 75-hour course before taking the state exam?

You can take the test at any time during the licensure process. It is better to take the exam upon completion of the qualifying courses. S*ince the 75-hour qualifying course prepares you for the questions on the state exam, it is recommended that you first complete the 75-hour course.*

7. Do I need broker sponsorship to take the New York State exam?

No. You may take the state exam and the 75-hour qualifying course without having a broker sponsor. Before taking the course or during the course, you should be looking for a broker to work for who will be your sponsor. This broker will sign and attest to sponsorship on your licensure application. When you submit your license application, this provides evidence of broker sponsorship. Since you can submit your application online through e*AccessNY*, the sponsoring broker can attest to sponsorship of your application online as well.

8. How often can I take these exams?

Depending on the policy of the entity conducting the 75-hour course, you can generally take one make-up exam if you do not pass the first time. Be sure to ask about this policy when you begin the course. If you pass the exam, you should apply for your license online utilizing your account in e*AccessNY*. If you fail the exam, you can schedule another exam by utilizing your account in e*AccessNY*. You can take the New York State exam as many times as you want.

9. If I do not wish to be licensed immediately, how long is my passing

   grade valid?

Passed exam results for the New York State are only valid for a period of two years.

10. Is there a fee for the state exam?

The fee is $15 for each time you take the exam. You must schedule a new online appointment to retake the exam.

11. What should I bring to the state exam?

1. Bring two #2 pencils. Calculators are permitted if they are battery or solar powered, silent, nonprinting and do not contain an alphabetic keyboard. PDA's are not allowed. You should bring a government-issued, signed, photo ID. Identification must be current and from the following list:
    - Driver's license
    - State-issued identification (ex, non-driver ID)
    - Military ID
    - United States Passport
    - United States INS issued ID
    - Certificate of US citizenship
2. You should also bring the page you were requested to print when you scheduled your exam on e*AccessNY*. This page is referred to as the "Summary of Your Submission" and includes all of your examination information, including your candidate number.

12. What kinds of questions are on the state exam?

All questions on the state exam are multiple-choice.

13. How many questions are there for each subject and what is the passing grade?

The numbers of questions on the classroom and state exams are weighted according to the number of hours allotted for each subject in the course. For example, agency law requires 11 classroom hours, so that topic will contain more exam questions than contracts that requires only one classroom hour. The qualifying course exam consists of 75 or 100 questions.

The state exam has 75 questions. Each question on the state exam is worth 1.33 points. The passing grade is 70 percent. The DOS "rounds downs" the grade, which means that you need a minimum of 52 correct questions to pass (which would also mean 23 wrong would give you a passing grade.) You have 1.5 hours to complete the exam.

14. Are all state exams the same?

Several different exams are developed from a large question bank. If you repeat the state exam, you probably will have a different set of questions.

15. Can I review my state licensure exam?

Yes, if you fail an exam, you may request an exam review. An exam review will help to evaluate your performance and the areas that require further study. You must request a review within 60 days of the examination date. You can ask for an Examination Review Request form at the exam and give the completed form to the Proctor. You can also call DOS to obtain one and then mail it back. You will have up to one hour for the review using your examination booklet and your answer sheet.

16. If I have equivalent real estate experience and plan to obtain a broker license, must I take the salesperson exam?

No. If you have prior experience, you may obtain broker licensure without first becoming a salesperson. You still must complete 120 hours of qualifying education; that is, the 75-hour salesperson course *and* the 45-hour broker-qualifying course. If you have taken the old 45-hour salesperson-qualifying course and not the current 75-hour salesperson-qualifying course, you will need to make up 30 hours. In this case, to obtain a broker license, you will need to complete a 30-hour remedial course in addition to the 45-hour broker-qualifying course. *This rule applies to all applicants for the broker license.*

Although you must pass the exams given with your qualifying (and/or remedial) courses, you need only take the broker state-licensing exam if you do not plan to obtain a salesperson license. In addition to the courses and passage of the exam, you must also demonstrate three years equivalent real estate experience.

17. How should I prepare for the exam?

If you have completed the 75-hour qualifying course, you already have studied all of the topics covered on your class and state exams, which is your primary preparation for the exam. After you complete the course, take some time to review your textbook and your notes. You should be familiar with the key terms, the important points and general theory, and the important laws pertaining to each subject. These items are summarized for you in *Cram for the Exam*.

Your completion of *Cram for the Exam* is an excellent final step in exam preparation.

Figure I.1 NYS Real Estate Licensure Exam Sites

ALBANY Exam Site
Alfred E. Smith State Office Building
80 South Swan Street
Albany, New York 12239
Located at the corner of Washington Avenue and South Swan Street

BINGHAMTON Exam Site (State Office Bldg.)
44 Hawley Street, 15th Floor
Binghamton, NY 13901

BUFFALO Exam Site (State Office Building)
65 Court Street
Main Floor Hearing Room, Part 5
Buffalo, NY 14202

FRANKLIN SQUARE Exam Site (VFW Hall)
68 Lincoln Road, Basement
Franklin Square, NY 11010

N6 Bus Route on Hempstead Turnpike
From the East, take the Southern State Parkway to Exit 16N, Franklin Ave.
From NYC/West, take the Cross Island Parkway SOUTH to the Southern State Parkway EAST. Take exit 15, Franklin Ave., turn left at the 2nd light onto Franklin Ave.
On Franklin Ave., turn RIGHT onto Hempstead Turnpike and go 5 blocks. Turn LEFT onto Lincoln Rd. (7-Eleven on corner). The VFW Hall and parking lot are on the RIGHT.

HAUPPAUGE Exam Site (Perry Duryea State Office Building)
250 Veterans Memorial Highway
Basement Conference Room
Hauppauge, NY 11788
Note: Building sits back off highway. Look for the green sign near the road.

NEW YORK CITY Exam Site
123 William Street, 19th Floor
New York, NY 10038

NEWBURGH Exam Site (Orange Ulster BOCES Adult Educational Center)
Federal Building, 471 Broadway, 2nd Floor
Newburgh, NY 12550
NYS Thruway Exit 17, take ramp toward Stewart Airport. Turn LEFT onto NY-17K, continue approximately 2 miles. Exam Site is on RIGHT.

PLATTSBURGH Exam Site (Clinton County Community College)
Lake Shore Drive, Route 9 South
Plattsburgh, NY 12901

ROCHESTER Exam Site (Finger Lakes DDSO)
620 Westfall Road
Rochester, NY 14620
Take NYS Thruway to Exit 46, take 390 North to exit 16, turn RIGHT on East Henrietta Road, turn right at 2nd traffic light onto Westfall Road, Finger Lakes DDSO is on LEFT. Park in lot on right. Do Not enter through main lobby. Look for Sign, "New York State Testing."

SYRACUSE Exam Site ***Broker Exam Only***
333 E. Washington Street, Main Floor, Hearing Room A
Syracuse, NY 13202

SYRACUSE Exam Site ***Salesperson Exam Only***
407 East Taft Road, (park in the rear of the building, enter through back door)
North Syracuse
Syracuse, NY 13212

UTICA Exam Site (State Office Bldg.)
207 Genesee Street 1st Floor, Room 107
Utica, NY 13501

WATERTOWN Exam Site (State Office Bldg.)
317 Washington Street, 11th Floor
Watertown, NY 13601

Source: New York State Department of State

Other Preparation Sources

Here are some other sources for your exam preparation:

➢ **New York Real Estate for Salespersons, 4th e.** This textbook completely covers the required New York syllabus for the 75-hour course. All of the questions in *Cram for the Exam* are referenced to this textbook so that you can easily find further clarification of your answer.

If you have not used this textbook in your course, have missed some classroom hours, or want to spend addition time studying, you may want to review this textbook. The book provides additional information on the licensure process in the Introductory Chapter and Chapter 1, "License Law and Regulations". The other items listed below provide supplementary review.

➢ *New York Real Estate for Brokers, 4th e.* This is the companion textbook to New York Real Estate for Salespersons. The textbook completely covers the required New York syllabus for the broker 45-hour course.

➢ *30 Hour Remedial Course Supplement.* This companion text for the salesperson or broker course is for students who have completed the old salesperson 45-hour course and need to complete the 75 hours for the salesperson course or the 120 hours for the broker course.

➢ *Cram for Exam: Your Guide to Passing the New York Broker Exam, 4th e.* This comprehensive review for the broker exam is similar in format to this exam guide.

➢ **Author website:** www.cramforexam.net. Marcia's website contains downloadable practice NYS licensing exams, other textbooks for sale, license requirements, and important information and updates for students and instructors.

Contact your Cengage Learning representative for ordering information

Phone: 1.888.248.5384

Proprietary school contact: Sheila Cole; Colleges and Universities contact: Michelle Kavanaugh

Web Info: http://academic.cengage.com/realestate/

Quick Tips to Help You Pass

Before the Exam

✓ Try to get a good night's sleep.

✓ Make sure you know the exact location of the test, and arrive there about one-half hour before the test begins.

✓ Take the necessary ID, pencils, calculator, and paperwork.

✓ Fear can be contagious; avoid pre-exam socializing and stay calm.

✓ If possible, sit toward the front of the examination room, where there are fewer distractions.

✓ Pay close attention to all instructions and follow them carefully.

✓ If you are physically challenged, you may call the Department of State (DOS) and have arrangements made to assist you with taking the exam.

During the Exam

Selecting an answer

✓ Answer every question as you go along. If you do not know an answer, take a guess or mark down the question number on scratch paper so you can return to it later. (DOS exam proctors collect all scratch paper after the exam.)

✓ Read the questions slowly and cautiously. The question may ask for a negative answer rather than a positive one. Do not read *into* the question; read it as it actually reads. Do not look for deeper hidden meanings. If you have studied, the first answer that occurs to you is generally the correct one.

✓ Read every answer before deciding on your choice.

✓ Note that questions usually contain two distracters (incorrect choices) that are obviously wrong. Spot them and you have a 50% chance of selecting the correct answer. There may be a third distracter that is not as obviously wrong as the others are, so if you eliminate all three, all that is left is the correct answer! Often you can find the correct answer through this process of elimination without actually knowing the correct answer.

✓ Do not always apply the maxim-"I cannot change my first answer." You may have initially misread the question. One word you may not have noticed before can change the meaning of the question upon rereading it.

✓ Watch out for "must" and "always". If an answer has any exceptions, these words generally indicate a wrong answer.

Timing Yourself

✓ Keep in mind that every question counts the same, so do not spend a lot of time on one complex question if it results in your running out of time. Finish the exam; then go back to the questions you either guessed at or could not answer.

✓ Use all of your allotted time. You have 1.5 hours to answer 75 multiple-choice questions. You might want to leave when you finish, but use this time to go back to the answers you are unsure of. By rereading a question, you might see it in an entirely different light.

✓ Before handing in your exam, carefully review all of your answers. If you spot just one wrong answer, it could make the difference between passing and failing.

✓ If you are still unsure of an answer, go with your first impression.

Marking Your Answer Sheet

✓ Make sure that your answer sheet is lined up correctly with each of the questions.

✓ If you erase, erase completely. The computerized test reader could pick up a faint mark.

✓ When marking answers you are certain of (and will not return to later), press down with the pencil on the answer sheet so that the test reader picks up the answer.

How to Cram for the Exam

1. First, review your textbook and any notes you have from your 75-hour qualifying course. Focus on areas where you had some difficulty.

2. Next, use the "Subject Review" section in this book to review the key terms and key points for the 18 qualifying course subjects that include 25 topics. The key terms included in this section are identical to the key terms required by the New York State syllabus for the salesperson-qualifying course. The key terms' section also include other items that you should know. Knowing the meaning of these key terms is essential, as you will see them repeatedly in exam questions.

3. If you have questions regarding key terms or key points, refer back to your textbook for further clarification. This cram book is best suited for use with *New York Real Estate for Salespersons, 4th e* by Marcia Darvin Spada. The textbook completely covers all material required for the state exam in an easy-to-understand format. See "Other Preparation Sources" earlier in this book for information on how to obtain a copy of the textbook.

4. Now, you are ready to begin your self-test review. "Questions for Your Review" contains 10 questions for each subject in the salesperson-qualifying course. When answering the review questions, pay attention to all choices. Even the wrong choices may be terms that will be on the state exam. If you do not know their meaning, look them up in the "Subject Review" or your textbook. Do not time yourself for this review. However, complete it under exam conditions, i.e., in a quiet place where you are not disturbed.

5. Use the Answer Key in the back of the book to grade your work. Then review the subject areas where your understanding is weak. The Answer Key provides an explanation for each question including a brief explanation of the correct and wrong answer choices. In addition, the Answer Key provides the page numbers in *New York Real Estate for Salespersons* where the material tested in each question is found. This allows you to find quickly the material in the textbook for further clarification. Keep in mind that sporadic wrong answers do not reflect weakness. You are doing quite well if you miss no more than 25 of the 250 questions in the review.

6. After you complete the review, complete Sample Practice Exams 1 and 2. These tests contain 75 questions just as the state exam does. The numbers of questions for each subject are similar to the state exam. The exams are based on information that you should know according to the New York syllabus. Be sure to take the Practice Exams under exam conditions. You should have no interruptions. You should allot yourself a maximum of 1.5 hours, just as in the state exam. The Answer Key provides the correct answers and the page numbers in *New York Real Estate for Salespersons* where the tested material can be found. There is also an explanation for each answer. If you do not pass these sample state exams, further study is needed. Check again the topics where you had wrong answers and re-study them. The exams are divided into topics so that you can easily see where you need further study. These sample exams are very good predictors of your performance on the state exam, so you should not attempt the state exam until you are comfortable with the material in this review.

A Word of Encouragement

The best guarantee for success on any exam is preparation. Your willingness to spend time working with *Cram for the Exam* will help you realize your goal. However, some people, no matter how well prepared, may not succeed on the first try. Many factors may come into play; how well you feel on that particular day, your level of anxiety, and sometimes just plain luck. Take care of the details that you can control, and try to relax. Most importantly, do not give up! If you do not pass on the first attempt, you have many resources available to help you succeed.

Disclaimer

The situations in the questions are fictional and the names of people and businesses are not related to real people or businesses. To simplify the text, the pronoun "he" is used to mean both male and female.

Subject Review

Review the key terms and key points for each subject before completing the 250-question review and sample exams. Instead of memorizing, strive for understanding. Additional terms and facts are fully explained in the textbook *New York Real Estate for Salespersons 4th e.* The following review of each chapter reinforces the information you should know for your exam and gives you an overview of the subject material. If you are still unsure of the subject after studying the review and completing the review questions for the topic, refer to the companion textbook.

License Law and Regulations

Key Terms

Apartment information vendor An individual who, for a fee, furnishes information about the location of residential real property, including apartments, that are available to be rented, shared, or sublet

Apartment sharing agent An individual who, for a fee, arranges and coordinates meetings between the current owners or occupants of real property, including apartments, who wish to share their housing with others

Article 12-A of the Real Property Law Contains most of the law pertaining to salespersons and brokers

Article 78 proceeding The method for judicial review of determinations by regulatory agencies such as DOS

Associate real estate broker A licensed real estate broker who may perform the acts performed by a broker, but by choice wants to work under the name and supervision of a licensed broker

Blind ads Ads placed by a broker that do not indicate that the advertiser is a broker and do not give the broker's name and telephone number

Commingling The mixing of others' funds, such as deposit money, with a broker's business or personal funds; brokers are prohibited from commingling funds

Escrow Account A fund deposited in an insured bank for the purpose of keeping deposit money

Kickback An improper payment by a broker or salesperson to someone who is not licensed or is not exempt from the license law; additionally, salespersons may not share a commission with other licensees

Misdemeanor A crime punishable by a fine of not more than $1,000 and/or imprisonment for not more than one year

Multiple Listing Service A system that pools the listings of all member companies

New York Department of State (DOS), Division of Licensing Services Governs the real estate licensure process and approves all real estate licenses

Pocket card A state-issued identification card that salespersons and brokers must carry in the course of business

Real estate broker   Any person, partnership, association, or corporation that, for another and for compensation of any kind, negotiates any form of real estate transaction; also supervises and accepts responsibility for the activities of sponsored associate brokers and salespersons

Real estate salesperson   One who performs any of the acts allowable under law by a real estate broker for compensation of any kind, but does so in association with and under the supervision of a licensed broker

Reciprocity   An arrangement in which nonresident salespersons and brokers licensed in another state must take the New York exam and maintain an office in New York, unless their home state does not require New York licensees to have an office in their state or pass their exam to practice real estate there

Revocation   Permanent removal of a license by the state

Sponsor   A broker that holds the license for the salesperson

Suspension   Temporary lifting of a license by the state for a designated time

Uniform Irrevocable Consent and Designation Form   Gives the New York courts jurisdiction over unlawful actions of the applicant while doing business in New York and allows summonses and other legal documents to be served on the New York Secretary of State in place of personal service on the applicant

Key Points

1. The purpose of license laws is to protect the public and elevate the standards of the real estate industry.
2. A real estate broker is a person or an organization that, for compensation of any kind, performs or offers to perform aspects of real estate transactions for others.
3. Real estate salespersons perform acts that a broker is authorized to perform, but they do so on behalf of a broker with whom they are associated.
4. Associate real estate brokers must fulfill the same requirements as a broker, but their status in the firm is the same as that of salespersons.
5. Attorneys do not need a license to practice real estate brokerage unless they employ licensees to work under their supervision.
6. The New York Department of State Division of Licensing Services oversees the licensure process.
7. The DOS has the power to deny, revoke, fine, or suspend a license.
8. The term of licensure for real estate salespersons and brokers is two years.
9. New York has reciprocal arrangements with other states for the licensure of nonresident licensees.
10. Other licenses and registrations related to real estate include mortgage bankers and mortgage brokers, apartment information vendors and apartment sharing agents, licensed or certified appraisers, and home inspectors.
11. Net listings, kickbacks, and commingling of funds are illegal. There are many other common violations of license law.
12. The DOS has specific guidelines for real estate advertising by licensees and for the employment and duties of unlicensed real estate assistants.

13. Violation of the license law is a misdemeanor and is punishable by a $1,000 fine and/or a maximum sentence of one year in jail.

14. The revocation or suspension of a broker's real estate license suspends the license of the salespersons and associate brokers in the broker's employ.

15. Licensees must inform sellers that a Property Condition Disclosure Statement is to be provided to the buyer or the buyer's agent before the sellers accept the purchase offer.

16. A seller must disclose to the buyer the existence of any known uncapped natural gas wells on the property. The seller must disclosure this information before he and the buyer enter into a contract of sale.

Law of Agency and Independent Contractor
Part I Law of Agency

Key Terms

Agency disclosure form Mandatory disclosure of representation form used for the sales or rental of residential one -to four unit properties

Agent When one person, the agent, agrees and is authorized to act on behalf of another person, the principal, an *agency relationship* is created

Brokerage The business of bringing buyers and sellers together and assisting in negotiations for the terms of sale of real estate

Broker's agent One who is engaged by a broker to work for that broker; in this relationship, the principal is not vicariously liable for the acts of any of the broker's agents; the broker who engaged these agents accepts this liability

Buyer agent One who represents the buyer of real property by entering into an agreement to work in the best interest of the buyer

Clayton Antitrust Act (1914) Supplements the Sherman Act and has the same general purpose; covers restraints on interstate trade or commerce not covered by the Sherman Act

Client The principal is also known as the agent's *client*

Cooperating agents Licensees from the same or other offices who participate as agents of buyers or sellers in a real estate transaction

Customer The party whom the agent brings to the principal as a seller, buyer, or tenant of a property

Designated agent A salesperson or an associate broker, supervised by a broker, who is assigned to represent a client when a different client is also represented by such real estate broker in the same transaction.

Disclosure and informed consent Explanation by a real estate agent of his position in the agency relationship and the verbal and written consent of the relationship for which the agency is created

Dual agent An agent who attempts to represent both the buyer and the seller in the same transaction; must have the written approval of both parties after the agent's informed disclosure that the buyer and seller each will relinquish the agent's duty of undivided loyalty in the fiduciary relationship

Estoppel An agency relationship created when an individual claims incorrectly that someone is his agent and a third party relies on the incorrect representation

Exclusive agency listing A listing with one broker as the only or *exclusive* agent; the broker is legally entitled to the commission agreed upon if the exclusive broker or another broker effects sale of the property, but not if the owner sells the property without the assistance of any broker

Exclusive right to sell A listing with one *exclusive* broker under which the broker is entitled to the commission no matter who effects the sale, including the owner

Express agency An agency relationship created by an oral or written agreement between the principal and agent

Fiduciary A position of trust; under a fiduciary relationship, the principal is owed faith, trust, and confidentiality by his agent

Fiduciary duties Reasonable care, skill and diligence obedience, accountability, loyalty and disclosure of information

First substantive meeting The first contact or meeting when some detail and information about the property is shared with parties who express some interest in the real estate transaction

General agent Someone authorized to handle all affairs of the principal concerning a specified matter or property, usually with some limited power to enter contracts

Group boycott A conspiracy in which a person or group is persuaded or coerced into not doing business with another person or group

Implied agency Creating an agency by words or actions of the principal and agent that indicate that they have an agency agreement

Market allocation agreement An agreement between competitors dividing or assigning a certain area or territory for sales

Net listing A listing contract that allows the broker to keep as a commission any money obtained from the sale above a sale price specified by the seller

Open listing agreement A listing with one or more brokers; any broker effecting the sale is entitled to the commission unless the owner sells the property

Price fixing A conspiracy by competitors in a group or industry to charge the same or similar price for services rendered

Principal The person who selects the agent to act on his behalf

Ratification The creation of an agency when a person claims to be an agent but has no express agreement, and the principal ratifies or accepts the agent's actions

Section 443 of the Real Property Law Requires that licensees present a written disclosure form that details consumer choices as to representation at the first substantive contact with a prospective seller or buyer; applies to the sales and rental of one- to four-unit residential properties; does not cover vacant land or condominium and cooperative apartments in buildings containing more than four units

Self Dealing Occurs when a broker has an undisclosed interest in a property

Seller agent A listing agent, an agent who cooperates with a listing agent as a seller's subagent, or a broker's agent who represents the owner of real property establishing a principal/client relationship to work in the seller's best interests

Sherman Antitrust Act (1890) Enacted to preserve a system of free economic enterprise and to protect the public against the activities of monopolies, contracts, or other combinations that unreasonably restrain trade

Single agent An agent who works only for the buyer or the seller and who may elect to reject subagency

Special agent An individual with narrow authorization to act on behalf of the principal; an example is a real estate broker who has a real estate listing

Subagents The principal's authorization of an agent to use other people to assist in accomplishing the purpose of the agency; these people are agents of the seller/principal and the broker with whom the property is listed

Tie-in arrangements Agreements between a party selling a product or service with a buyer that, as a condition of the sale, the buyer will buy something from the seller or the buyer will not buy the other's product or service

Undivided loyalty Loyalty to the principal only

Undisclosed dual agency A situation in which an agent represents the seller and the buyer in the same transaction but does not disclose his position

Vicarious liability One person is responsible or liable for the actions of the other. According to Section 442-c of the New York Real Property Law, a broker's license may be revoked or suspended for a salesperson's actions if the broker had actual knowledge of such violation or if the broker retains the benefits from the transaction after he knows that the salesperson has engaged in some wrongdoing.

Key Points

1. When buyers or sellers of real estate hire a licensee to act on their behalf, they create an agency relationship. An agreement (express agency) usually creates an agency relationship. However, the relationship can be implied by the agent's conduct. A position of trust, which is a fiduciary relationship, exists between every principal and agent in an agency relationship.
2. Real estate agents are special agents with specific authority.
3. The agent's fiduciary duties and responsibilities include obedience; loyalty; disclosure of information; confidentiality; accountability; and reasonable care, skill, and diligence.
4. A brokerage contract is created when the principal, usually a real estate owner, hires a broker (agent) to perform services relating to the real estate. Every agency relationship is consensual.
5. The principal can authorize the agent to use other people to assist in accomplishing the purpose of the agency. These people are subagents.

6. The nature of the compensation (commission or flat fee) (or the person who pays it) does not determine the agency relationship.

7. An agent may decide to represent the seller or the buyer in a real estate transaction.

8. A single agent works only for the buyer or seller directly and may elect to reject subagency.

9. A seller agent represents the owner of real property. The seller agent accepts the employment contract of a listing agreement, establishing a client relationship in the seller's best interest.

10. A buyer agent represents the buyer/purchaser of real property. The buyer agent accepts the employment contract of a listing agreement, establishing a client relationship in the buyer's best interests.

11. A dual agent is an agent who attempts to represent the buyer and the seller in the same transaction. Dual agency occurs in real estate companies when the firm attempts to represent both the buyer and the seller in the same transaction.

12. According to New York law, an alternative for handling a dual agency in a brokerage firm is the designated sales associate or agent. With disclosure and informed consent, one sales agent in the firm is designated to represent the buyer. Another agent is designated to represent the seller.

13. A multiple listing service (MLS) offers cooperation and compensation to participating members. It does not create an automatic subagency.

14. Cooperating agents are seller agents from another real estate firm acting as subagents of the listing broker and seller. Cooperative agents are also buyer agents from another real estate firm. These agents work through the usual system of offerings published within an MLS.

15. In the sale or rental of one- to four-unit residential properties in New York, a dual agent must have the *written* approval of both parties after the agent's informed disclosure. The buyer and the seller each agree to relinquish the individual, undivided loyalty in the fiduciary relationship.

16. An undisclosed dual agency can result in a violation of New York Real Property Law.

17 New York real estate firms can provide consensual dual agency for in-house sales.

18. All agents must disclose what party they represent in a real estate transaction.

19. In the sale or rental of one- to four-unit residential properties in New York, the agent must present a mandatory disclosure form to all parties signing listing agreements. The form is also presented at other meetings and discussions between prospective buyers and sellers at the first substantive contact or meeting.

20. There are two separate agency disclosure forms: NYS Disclosure Form for Buyer and Seller and NYS Disclosure Form for Landlord and Tenant.

Law of Agency and Independent Contractor
Part II Independent Contractor

Key Terms

Employee Employment status in which the employer must withhold federal, state, and social security (FICA) taxes and use special reporting forms; employee is supervised by employer

Independent contractor A work situation in which the employer does not have the right to control the details of a worker's performance; form 1099 misc. is filed with IRS indicating the worker's yearly income

Key Points

1. The IRS code classifies real estate salespersons and brokers as independent contractors. To qualify, the real estate agent must be licensed and the broker and the sales associate enter into a written contract.
2. As independent contractors, licensees do not receive sick pay or medical benefits and must file a Form 1099-MISC with IRS. They pay self-employment taxes.

Legal Issues
Part I Estates and Interests

Key Terms

Act of waste When a life tenant abuses or misuses a property

Air rights Rights to the area above the earth

Beneficiary One who receives benefits or gifts from the acts of others given, for example, by a will or trust

Bundle of rights A visual concept that illustrates interests in and title to real property, including air rights, water rights, mineral rights, easements, leases, and mortgages

Chattel Another name for personal property

Defeasible fee A title subject to being lost if certain conditions occur

Dower and curtesy An automatic life estate owned by a surviving spouse in inheritable property owned by the deceased spouse alone during the marriage; for practical purposes, not valid in New York

Estate in real property An interest in the property sufficient to give the holder of the estate the right to possession

Fee simple absolute This estate provides the most complete form of ownership and bundle of rights in real property

Fee simple on condition A fee simple defeasible ownership recognized by the words "but if" in the transfer

Fixtures Improvements both on and to the land

Freehold estate Ownership for an undetermined length of time

Holdover tenant A tenant who does not leave upon expiration of the lease

Illiquidity Investments in which one's assets are not readily convertible to cash

Joint tenancy A form of co-ownership requiring all four unities of time, title, interest, and possession

Leasehold estate An estate of less than a lifetime and therefore of limited duration

Life estate Possession and control for the remainder of someone's life

Littoral rights Rights that apply to property bordering a nonflowing body of water, such as a lake or sea

Parcel A specific portion of land, such as a lot

Partition A legal proceeding dividing property of co-owners so each will hold title in severalty or directing that the property be sold and the proceeds be divided

Periodic estate An estate that renews itself for another period at the end of each period unless one party gives notice to the other during the prescribed time

Personal property Everything that is not real property

Qualified fee simple A fee simple defeasible estate recognized by the words "as long as" in the deed

Real estate Land and all improvements, whether found in nature or placed there by people

Real property Real estate plus all legal rights, powers, and privileges inherent in ownership

Reversionary interest Upon the death of a life tenant, the reversion of possession to the grantor or the grantor's heirs, if no other specification has been made

Right of survivorship When one (or more) of the co-owners of a property dies, the right of surviving co-owners to the interest of the deceased

Riparian water rights Rights that belong to owners of property bordering a flowing body of water

Severalty Title to real property held in the name of only one person or entity; the interest is *severed* from all others

Special purpose property Property that combines both the land and improvements for one highest and best use, such as a public park

Subsurface rights Rights to the area below the earth's surface; also called *mineral rights*

Tenancy in common Tenancy characterized by two or more persons holding title to a property at the same time; the only required unity is that of the right to possession

Tenants by the entirety Form of ownership limited to husband and wife; contains the right of survivorship

Trade fixtures Items installed by a commercial tenant and removable upon termination of the tenancy

Trust A fiduciary relationship between the trustee and the beneficiary of the trust

Trustee One who holds title to property for the benefit of a beneficiary

Trustor One who conveys title to a trustee

Unity of interest Co-owners who all have the same percentage of ownership in a property

Unity of possession Co-owners who have the right to possess or access any portion of a property that is owned without physical division

Unity of time Co-owners who receive title at the same time in the same conveyance

Unity of title Co-owners who have the same type of ownership, such as a life estate, fee simple, or conditional fee

Key Points

1. Real property consists of land and everything attached to the land and the bundle of rights inherent in ownership.
2. Everything that is not real property is personal property.
3. Ownership in land includes the surface of the earth and the area above and below the surface, although these rights may be assigned.
4. Personal property that attaches permanently to the land or improvements and becomes part of the real property is a fixture.
5. Real property has the physical characteristics of immobility, indestructibility, and uniqueness and economic characteristics based on scarcity, permanence of investment, location, and improvements.
6. Estates in land are divided into two groups: freehold estates and estates of less than freehold (nonfreeholds or leaseholds).
7. Freehold estates are fee simple estates that are inheritable. Freehold estates are also life estates that are not inheritable.
8. The most complete form of ownership in real property is fee simple absolute.
9. Life estates may be in reversion or in remainder. The duration of a life estate may be measured by the life tenant or by the life of another (pur autre vie). A life tenant has the right of possession and enjoyment of the property. He has the right to derive certain income from it.
10. Title held in the name of one person only is ownership in severalty.
11. When two or more people or organizations hold title at the same time, it is called co-ownership or concurrent ownership. The forms of co-ownership include tenancy in common, joint tenancy, tenancy by the entirety, and community property.
12. Joint tenancy and tenancy by the entirety include the right of survivorship and require the unities of time, title, interest, and possession. Tenancy by the entirety is restricted to husband and wife.
13. Business organizations may receive, hold, and convey title to real property.

Legal Issues
Part II Liens and Easements

Key Terms

Appurtenances Inherent or automatic ownership rights that are a natural consequence of owning real property

Corporation franchise tax A tax calculated on the net profit of the corporation, which if not paid, becomes a lien against the corporation's assets

Dominant tenement The land that benefits from an easement appurtenant or from an easement in gross

Easement A nonpossessory interest in land owned by another; someone who owns an easement right does not own or possess the land where the easement lies, only the right to a specified use

Easement appurtenant All easements that are not easements in gross; two land owners must be involved, one receiving a benefit and the other accepting a burden

Easement by condemnation Created by the exercise of the government's right of eminent domain

Easements by grant or reservation Created by the express written agreement of the land owners, usually in a deed

Easements by implication Arises by implication from the conduct of the parties

Easements by necessity Exists when land has no access to roads and is landlocked

Easements by prescription Obtained by use of the land of another for a legally prescribed length of time

Easement for light and air A type of negative easement generally pertaining to the view of a property

Easements in gross Also called commercial easements in gross; usually owned by a government agency, or a public utility

Encroachment A trespass on the land of another created by the intrusion of some structure or object, such as a tree limb or roof overhang, across a boundary line

Encumbrance Interest in a property that secures debt or gives use and/or control to another

General liens Claims against all property of a debtor

In rem legal proceeding A legal action brought against the real property and not against an individual and his personal property

Involuntary lien A lien created by a legal proceeding when a creditor places a claim on real and/or personal property to obtain payment of a debt

Judgment A court decree resulting from a lawsuit

License Permission to do a particular act or series of acts on land of another without possessing any estate or interest in the land

Lien A claim or charge against the property of another

Lis pendens A notice that a lawsuit has been filed and a trial is pending, the judgment in which will affect title to a specific property

Materialman's lien A specific lien filed by a supplier of products required in construction or improvement of a building

Mechanic's lien A specific lien filed by a person who provides labor or furnishes material for the improvement of real property

Nonpossessory A non ownership interest in a property such as an easement

Party wall A common wall used by two adjoining structures

Possessory Either actively or constructively occupy the property which gives the possessor certain rights

Profit The right to take products of the soil from the land of another

Restrictive covenant Restrictions placed on a private owner's use of land by a nongovernmental entity or an individual

Servient tenement The land that suffers by allowing an easement use

Specific lien Claims, such as a mortgage, against a specific and readily identifiable property

Voluntary lien A lien in which individuals consent to placing a charge against their property as security for a debt; a mortgage is an example of a voluntary lien

Writ of attachment A court order preventing any transfer of the attached property during the litigation

Key Points

1. An encumbrance is a claim, lien, charge, or liability attached to and binding upon real property. Examples are encroachments, easements, leases, liens, assessments, and restrictive covenants.
2. Specific liens are claims against a specific and readily identifiable property, such as a mortgage or a mechanic's lien.
3. The lien for real property taxes is a specific lien. In New York, this lien has the highest priority for payment.
4. Mechanics' and materialmen's liens are specific liens that may receive preferential treatment for priority of liens.
5. A lis pendens notice provides specific and constructive public notice that a lawsuit affecting title or possession of certain real estate is pending.
6. General liens are claims against a person and all of his property, such as a judgment resulting from a lawsuit. The property of a judgment debtor is subject to execution and forced sale to satisfy an unpaid judgment.
7. Easements are nonpossessory interests in land owned by another. Easements can be in gross or appurtenant. Easements are created by grant (reservation), necessity, prescription, implication, and condemnation.
8. Easements appurtenant can be negative or affirmative.
9. Easements are terminated by release, merger, abandonment, necessity, or expiration of the prescribed time.
10. An encroachment is a trespass on land or an intrusion over the boundary of land. A survey of a boundary provides evidence of an encroachment.
11. A profit in real property is transferable and inheritable. A license in real property is not transferable or inheritable.

Legal Issues
Part III Deeds

Key Terms

Accession Real property owners' right to all that their land produces or all that is added to the land, either intentionally or by mistake

Accretion The gradual building up of land in a watercourse over time by deposits of silt, sand, and gravel

Acknowledgment Public officer or notary's witnessing of signatures that make a deed or other instrument eligible for recording; the signatory must appear before a public officer, such as a notary public, and state that signing the deed was a voluntary act

Administrator (man) or Administratrix (woman) The person appointed by a court to distribute the property of a person dying intestate

Adverse possession A method of acquiring title to real property by conforming to statutory requirements; a form of involuntary alienation of title

Alluvion The land mass added to property over time by accretion; owned by the owner of the land to which it has been added

Avulsion The loss of land when a sudden or violent change in a watercourse results in its washing away

Bargain and sale deed May be with or without covenants of warranty; with covenants, the grantor claims that he is conveying substantial title and possession of the property; without covenants, the legal effect is similar to a quitclaim deed

Beneficiary or legatee The recipient of a gift of personal property by will

Bequest or legacy A gift of personal property by will

Conveyance A deed

Codicil A supplement or appendix to a will either adding or changing some bequest

Dedication A gift of land or an easement for public use; an example of an implied dedication is when the public is allowed access to a private road

Dedication by deed Used when a developer deeds to the municipality a parcel of land for a park; a cession or quitclaim deed may be used

Deed The document used to legally convey title to real property

Deed of correction Used when a deed contains an error that requires correction

Deed of gift Conveys real property without consideration; can be accomplished by any type of deed

Deed of trust A conveyance of real property that gives legal title to a trustee; not commonly used in New York, it can take the place of a mortgage because the title gives security for repayment of the debt owed on the property

Delivery and acceptance To effect transfer of title by transfer a deed, the grantor must deliver a deed to the grantee and the grantee must accept the deed

Description by monument Used in place of the metes and bounds method when describing multiple-acre tracts of land that would be very expensive to survey; permanent objects such as stone walls, large trees, or boulders are used as markers

Description by reference, plat, or lot and block Legal description that references a plat of subdivision or other legal document

Devise A gift of real property by will

Devisee A recipient of the gift of real property by will

Executor (man) or Executrix (woman) A person appointed in a will to carry out its provisions

Formal or witnessed will One signed by the testator or testatrix in front of two witnesses where he declares the writing to be his last Will and Testament and states that it expresses his wishes for the disposition of his property after death

Full covenant and warranty deed Contains the strongest and broadest form of guarantee of title of any type of deed and therefore the greatest protection to the grantee

Grantee The person receiving title; does not need to have legal capacity; a minor or a mentally incompetent person can receive and hold title to real property

Granting clause The essential clause in a deed, containing words of conveyance stating that it is the grantor's intention to transfer the title to the named grantee

Grantor The one conveying the title; must be legally competent

Guardian's deed A deed executed by an individual who is legally vested with the power to manage the rights and property of another

Habendum clause A clause in a deed beginning with the words, *to have and to hold*, which describes the estate granted and always must agree with the granting clause

Intestate The condition of death without leaving a valid will

Involuntary alienation Occurs when an individual must relinquish title to real property against her will

Judicial deed Results from a court order to the official executing the deed; contain no warranties

Land patent Instrument conveying public land to a private party; can also mean the actual land conveyed

Metes and bounds description Legal description of surveyed land where the metes are the distances from point to point in the description and the bounds are the directions from one point to another

Probate Judicial determination of a will's validity by a court of competent jurisdiction and subsequent supervision over distribution of the estate

Public grant A grant of a power, license, or real property from the state or government to a private individual

Quitclaim deed Simply a deed of release; releases or conveys to the grantee any interest, including title, that the grantor may have; contains no warranties

Referee's deed An instrument executed by an individual empowered by the court to exercise judicial power, as in a court-ordered sale and conveyance of real property

Reference to a plat A valid legal description on a deed referring to a plat (map) and lot number as part of a recorded subdivision

Reliction An increase in land by the permanent withdrawal of a sea, river, lake, stream, or other body of water

Sheriff's deed Gives ownership rights in property to a buyer at a sheriff's sale

Testate A person who dies having made a valid will while alive; a person may die testate as to some property and intestate as to other property

Testator A man who makes a will; a woman is a testatrix

Voluntary alienation Willing transfer of title during life; accomplished by the grantor's delivery of a valid deed to the grantee while both are alive

Key Points

1. A deed is the document used to convey title to real property. Transfer of title is termed *alienation*. Alienation may be voluntary or involuntary.
2. The requirements for deed validity are (1) deed in writing, (2) competent grantor, (3) competent or incompetent grantee, (4) grantor and grantee named with certainty, (5) adequate property description, (6) recital of consideration, (7) words of conveyance that sometimes contain a habendum clause, (8) proper execution by grantor, and (9) delivery and acceptance to convey title.
3. To be eligible for recording on the public record, a deed must be acknowledged or proved. Recording protects the grantee's title against future conveyances by the grantor.
4. Deed descriptions include metes and bounds, lot and block (plat of subdivision), and monuments.
5. A full covenant and warranty deed is the strongest and broadest form of title guarantee.
6. A quitclaim deed is a deed of release and contains no warranties. It conveys any interest the grantor may have. The quitclaim deed is used mainly to remove a cloud from a title.
7. A bargain and sale deed may be with or without covenants. When the bargain and sale deed contains covenants, it is acceptable to lenders.
8. Judicial deeds result from a court order to the official executing the deed. Forms of judicial deeds include sheriff's deed, referee's deed, tax deed, guardian's deed, and executor's or administrator's deed.

9. When a person dies and leaves no will, the laws of descent determine the order of distribution of property to the heirs.
10. When a person dies and leaves a will, the gift of real property through the will is a devise. A gift of personal property through a will is a bequest.
11. Dedication occurs when land or an easement to land is given for public use.
12. A person other than the owner can claim title to real property under adverse possession. In New York, the possession must be continuous and uninterrupted for a period of ten years and a court must award title.

Legal Issues
Part IV Title Closing and Costs

Key Terms

Abstract of title A condensed history of the title, summarizing all links in the chain of title plus any other matters of public record affecting the title

Actual notice Requires that the person actually knows about a document or situation

Assessments Referring to condominiums and cooperatives monies payable to the homeowner's association for maintenance of the common elements

Certificate of title opinion An attorney's written opinion as to which person or entity owns a property and the quality of title and exceptions, if any, to clear title

Chain of title The successive conveyances of title, starting with the current deed and going back an appropriate time (typically 40 to 60 years); title must be unbroken to be good and, therefore, marketable

Closing statement Sets forth the distribution of monies involved in the transaction—who is to pay what amount for each expense and who is to receive that amount

Combined Real Estate Transfer Tax Return, Credit Line Mortgage Certificate, and Certification of Exemption from the Payment of Estimated Personal Income Tax Form (Form TP 584) This form is used to transmit the New York State transfer tax and is furnished by the NYS Department of Taxation and Finance. In addition to the transfer tax information and payment, the form includes other important sections.

Constructive notice The theory that all the world is bound by knowledge of the existence of a document if evidence of the document is recorded

Credit In a closing statement, money to be received or credit given for money

Debit In a closing statement, an expense; monies that are owed

Insurable title A title that is acceptable to a title insurance company

Marketable title One that is reasonably free and clear of encumbrances

Mortgage recording tax 0.75% percent of the mortgage amount in certain counties; in counties with a public transportation system, the amount is 1 percent, with 0.25 percent paid by the lender, if there is one

New York City Real Property Transfer Tax In addition to the New York State transfer tax, New York City imposes an additional transfer tax of 1 percent of the selling price for residential property; if the selling price is over $500,000, the transfer tax is 1.425%. For other property types, the tax is 1.425% and if the consideration is more than $500,000, the tax is 2.65%

Proration A division of closing costs to ensure fair apportioning of expenses between buyer and seller

Real Estate Settlement Procedures Act (RESPA) Applies to residential federally financed properties, not to commercial properties or to owner-financed loans, and regulates lending institutions in making mortgage loans

Real property transfer tax A tax on the conveyance of title to real property paid by the seller and based on the consideration the seller receives for the property

Real Property Transfer Report Used to document the information associated with all real property transfers within New York (Form RP-5217)

Survey The process by which parcels of land are measured; the final document is a map showing measurements, boundaries, and area

Title Evidence of the right to possess property

Title closing Settlement of the obligations undertaken in the contract of sale; parties to the title transfer and other interested persons review the closing documents, execute the closing documents, pay and receive money, and receive title

Title insurance policy A contract that insures the policy owner against financial loss if title to real estate is not good

Title search Search of the records affecting real estate titles

Key Points

1. At a title closing, all interested parties meet to review closing documents and to transfer title to real estate. The deed is the document that conveys the title from seller to purchaser (grantor to grantee).
2. Recordation of a deed provides protection for the owner's title against subsequent claimants. Deeds and other closing documents are recorded in the county clerk's office of the county where the property is situated; in New York City, they are recorded in the Office of the City Register.
3. The purpose of a title examination is to determine a title's quality. An attorney or a title company makes the examination. Only an attorney can legally give an opinion about the title's quality.
4. A title insurance policy protects the insured against financial loss caused by a title defect.
5. Various types of tests and inspections of the property take place before closing. A licensed home inspector accompanied by the purchaser generally performs the "structural" before (and sometimes after) a contract is signed. A real estate agent may take a prospective purchaser to a walk-through of the property immediately before closing.
6. The Real Estate Settlement Procedures Act (RESPA) regulates lending activities of lending institutions that provide mortgages for housing.

7. The closing statement computes the distribution of monies involved in the transaction.

8. Seller closing costs may include the New York title transfer taxes; broker commission; attorney fees; costs of document preparation; and satisfaction of existing liens, if any.

9. Purchaser costs may include the structural inspection; title search and title policy; survey fees; mortgage recording tax; lender fees; recording fees; and if relevant, broker commission.

10. Prorations are the division of expenses and income between the purchaser and the seller at closing.

The Contract of Sale and Leases
Part I Leases

Key Terms

Actual eviction Wrongful use of self-help whereby the landlord, without the aid or control of the court system, physically removes the tenant and his belongings from the premises or takes action to prevent tenant access to the premises

Assignment Transfer of a lease from the present tenant to the assignee; the assignee then must make lease payments to the landlord

Constructive eviction Occurs when the tenant is prevented from the quiet enjoyment of the premises

Estate at sufferance Describes a tenant who is originally in lawful possession of another's property but refuses to leave after his right to possession terminates

Estate at will An estate in which the duration of the term is unknown when the estate is created because either party may terminate the lease simply by giving notice to the other party

Estate for years Exists for a fixed period, which can be as short as one day

Eviction A legal action for removal of a tenant and his belongings and a return of possession of the premises to the landlord

Graduated lease One in which the rental changes from period to period over the lease term

Gross lease Provides for the owner (lessor) to pay all expenses, such as real property taxes, owner's insurance, liability insurance, and maintenance

Ground lease A long term lease of unimproved land, usually for construction purposes

Holdover tenant A tenant who remains in possession of a property after a lease terminates

Index lease A method of determining rent on long term leases where the rent is tied to an economic indicator such as an index

Landlease Allows a lessee the right to use land for any purpose for a specified period

Lease A contract in which, for a consideration (usually rent), a property owner transfers to a tenant a property interest or possession, for a prescribed time

Lessee The tenant placed in possession of the leased premises

Lessor The landlord or owner of the leased property

Net lease The tenant (lessee) pays some or all of the expenses

Percentage lease A lease with a base rent plus an additional monthly rent based on a percentage of the lessee's gross sales

Periodic lease Automatically renews itself for another period at the end of each period unless one party gives notice to the other at the prescribed time

Periodic tenancy or estate from year-to-year The period length can be a week, a month, or any other negotiated time period

Security deposit Money paid by the tenant at the start of a lease that will be refunded at the end of the lease based upon the condition of the premises; often negotiated as one month's rent

Sublease A lease under which a tenant leases a property to a third party, the sublessee; the original tenant is still responsible to the landlord for the lease payments under the original lease contract; the sublessee pays the rent to the tenant (lessee), and the tenant pays the landlord

Triple net lease In addition to the rent, the lessee pays all expenses associated with the property

Key Points

1. A contract between the landlord of property and the tenant creates a lease. The landlord is the lessor. The tenant is the lessee.
2. The landlord and tenant are bound by contractual rights and obligations created by the lease agreement.
3. Leasehold estates (or nonfreeholds) are estates of limited duration, providing possession and control but not title, as in the case of freehold estates. Leasehold estates are estates for years, periodic tenancy (estates from year to year), estates at will, and estates at sufferance.
4. The lessee's transfer of the entire remaining term of a lease is an assignment. A transfer of part of the lease term with a reversion to the lessee or a transfer of part of the leased premises is a subletting.
5. The Emergency Tenants Protection Act of 1974 (revised 1997) and several other laws govern rent regulation. Two programs, rent control and rent stabilization, are intended to protect tenants in privately owned buildings from illegal rent increases while limiting the rights of landlords to evict tenants.
6. In a lease of residential property, the landlord's warranty of habitability must provide habitable premises to the tenant.
7. At expiration of the lease, the tenant has a duty to maintain and return the premises to the landlord in the same condition as at the beginning of the lease, ordinary wear and tear excepted.
8. The tenant can make a claim of constructive eviction when the premises become uninhabitable because of the landlord's lack of maintenance. A determination of constructive eviction terminates the lease.

9. Leases terminate by (a) expiration of lease term, (b) mutual agreement, (c) breach of condition, (d) actual eviction, (e) court-ordered eviction, or (f) constructive eviction. Actual eviction is illegal in New York.

10. The two main classifications of leases based on arrangement for payment are the gross lease and the net lease. Under a gross lease, the landlord pays the real property taxes, insurance, and costs for maintaining the property. Under a net lease, the tenant pays some or all of these expenses.

11. Types of commercial leases are the percentage lease, the index lease, and the graduated payment lease.

12. A ground lease is a long-term lease on unimproved land. It is generally for construction purposes.

The Contract of Sale and Leases
Part II Contracts

Key Terms

Apportionment The division of expenses between seller and purchaser

Arm's length The relationship between parties to a contract; they are assumed to have equal bargaining power and are not related by business interest or familial relationship

As is Wording on an offer to purchase contract indicating that the premises is sold without warranty as to condition and the purchaser agrees to take title in the present condition subject to reasonable use, wear, and tear between the date of the contract and the closing date

Assignment A new party to a contract agrees to satisfy the former contracting party's obligation

Bilateral contract One in which two parties have made promises of some kind to each other

Binder In certain areas of New York, a written document for the purchase and sale of real property used by licensees instead of an offer to purchase contract; does not generally contain all the elements of a valid contract; however, if it does, it may be enforced as a contract

Caveat Latin for a warning or caution; in New York, properties that lie within an Agricultural District must have a disclosure attached stating that the property lies within an agricultural district

Caveat emptor Latin for "let the buyer beware"

Contingencies Additions, amendments or agreements annexed to the contract and incorporated into its terms

Contract An agreement between competent legal parties to do or refrain from doing some legal act in exchange for consideration

Counteroffer An acceptance that differs in any way from the offer

Earnest-money deposit Shows the sincerity of the buyer and expresses a commitment to raise the money called for in the contract

Executed contract A contract that has been fully performed

Executory contract A contract that is not fully performed

Express contract A contract in which the parties have agreed on all terms; can be written or oral

Forbearance May be granted by a lending institution; the act of refraining from taking legal action for nonpayment of a mortgage despite the fact that it is due

Implied contract One inferred from the conduct and actions of another without express agreement

Liquidated damages The parties to the contract can stipulate in the contract an amount of money to be paid upon certain breaches of the contract

Meeting of the minds When the parties to the contract reach agreement on the terms to be included in the contract

Novation A form of agreement that terminates a previous contract; the substitution of a new contract for a prior contract or the substitution of a new party for an old party

Offer to purchase contract A bilateral, express contract that is the "road map" for the real estate transaction

Option A contract in which an optionor (owner) sells a right to purchase a property to a prospective buyer, called an optionee, at a particular price for a specified time period; if no time limit is set, it may contain a clause allowing the optionee the first choice to either purchase or not purchase the property (right of first refusal) if a third party wishes to purchase the property

Power of attorney The right given by one party to another to perform certain acts in his behalf

Rescission To take back, remove, or annul; contract remedy applied when a contract has not been performed by either party and has been breached by a party

Specific performance An order from the court requiring the contract to be completed as originally agreed

Statute of limitations Law stating that, if a party to a contract fails to bring a lawsuit against a defaulting party within a time period set by statute, the injured party loses the right of remedy

"Time is of the essence" If written on the contract for purchase and sale, the closing must take place on or before the exact date stipulated in the contract

Unenforceable contract One that appears to meet the requirements for validity but would not be enforceable in court

Uniform Commercial Code Contains rules governing the financing of loans to purchase cooperative apartments; provides for the lender to retain a security interest in the personal property until the lender is paid in full

Unilateral contract When one party makes a promise in order to induce a second party to do something; the party making the promise is not obligated under the contract until the other party does what has been asked

Valid contract One that is binding and enforceable on all parties; contains all the essential elements of a contract

Voidable contract May or may not be enforceable between the parties; results from the failure of the contracting parties to meet some legal requirement in negotiating the agreement

Void contract Has absolutely no legal force or effect

Key Points

1. A contract is an agreement between competent parties, upon legal consideration, to do or refrain from doing some legal act.
2. An express contract is spoken or written. An implied contract is a contract inferred from the actions of the parties.
3. Bilateral contracts are based on mutual promises. Unilateral contracts are based on a promise by one party and an act by another party.
4. An executed contract is fully performed. An executory contract contains provisions yet to be performed.
5. A contract is created by the unconditional acceptance of a valid offer. Acceptance of bilateral offers must be communicated.
6. A voidable contract is one that may not be enforceable at the option of one of the parties to the contract.
7. The requirements for contract validity are (a) competent parties, (b) mutual agreement, (c) lawful objective, (d) consideration, and (e) written format when required to be.
8. The Statute of Frauds, which in New York is written into the General Obligations Law, requires that real estate contracts be in writing. Leases and listing contracts for more than one year must be in writing.
9. The remedies for breach of contract are (a) compensatory damages, (b) liquidated damages, (c) specific performance, and (d) rescission.
10. A sales contract is a road map for the real estate transaction and is a bilateral express contract.
11. A binder and an offer to purchase are written outlines of the scope of a real estate transaction. They may contain all of the essential elements of a valid contract.
12. An installment land contract is a sales contract and a method of financing by the seller for the buyer. Legal title does not pass until the buyer pays all or some specified part of the purchase price.
13. An option is often tied to a lease. In some cases, all or part of the rent applies toward the purchase price of the property.
14. A broker is generally entitled to a commission when he produces a buyer who is ready, willing, and able to purchase the subject property on terms acceptable to the seller.

The Contract of Sale and Leases
Part III Contract Preparation

Key Terms

Attorney review or approval clause A condition making a contract subject to approval by each party's attorney.

Down payment The portion of a property's purchase price that is paid in cash and is not part of the mortgage loan. In certain upstate areas, the term used is deposit down payment; generally, when the buyer defaults, the down payment is the amount of liquidated damages to which the seller is entitled.

Lawyers' Fund for Client Protection One of its purposes is to reimburse client money that is misused in the practice of law.

Mortgage contingency clause States that the closing is contingent, or dependent upon, the purchaser's receipt of a mortgage commitment.

Key Points

1. Contract preparation differs between upstate and downstate New York.
2. In many upstate counties, the real estate agent fills out a preprinted contract of sale. In other places, such as the downstate area, the agent prepares a binder or an offer to purchase. An attorney prepares the contract of sale.
3. A binder is also called a receipt, a purchaser offer, and an agreement. The real estate agent may prepare a binder. Downstate the seller's attorney sometimes prepares the binder.
4. Forms of contracts include the Contract of Sale (residential one- to four-unit property); Condominium Contract of Sale; Cooperative Contract of Sale; Commercial Contract of Sale for residential income property; Commercial Contract of Sale for retail, business property, and large tracts of land; Installment Sales Contract; and Option to Buy.
5. At the listing presentation, the agent can collect from the sellers the prior deed and title insurance policy; survey; CO; and property tax, fuel, and water bills. These documents assist the attorneys who are preparing the closing documents.
6. Generally, for a residential or commercial sale of improved property, the property's common address (street address) is used. When tracts of unimproved land or lots are transferred, the deed, tax map, plat map filed, or survey may be attached to the contract.
7. The mortgage contingency clause states that the closing is contingent, or dependent upon, the purchaser's receipt of a mortgage commitment. If the purchaser complies with the terms of the clause but does not obtain a commitment, the contract may be canceled and the deposit returned.
8. It is customary for a purchaser to deposit up to 10 percent of the purchase price, in escrow, as an initial contract down payment. However, this percentage or the amount can be negotiated between the parties.
9. One of the purposes of the Lawyers' Fund for Client Protection is to reimburse client escrow money that is misused by attorneys.
10. Generally, the purchaser signs the contract of sale first because the purchaser is the one making the offer. The purchaser is stating the purchase price he wants to offer and the terms.
11. A real estate agent who prepares a simple fill-in-the-blanks purchase and sale contract can avoid the unlawful practice of law by including in the contract a condition making it subject to approval by each party's attorney. This condition is contained in an attorney approval clause.
12. The New York Judiciary Law prohibits the practice of law by non-attorneys. A violation is a misdemeanor. The DOS can also take action against the licensee.

Real Estate Finance

Key Terms

Acceleration clause A mortgage clause enabling the lender to declare the entire balance remaining immediately due and payable if the borrower is in default

Adjustable rate mortgage (ARM) A mortgage interest rate that varies, depending on fluctuations of a standard financial index

Alienation (due-on-sale) clause A clause in the note accompanying a mortgage that entitles the lender to declare the principal balance immediately due and payable if the borrower sells the property during the mortgage term; makes the mortgage unassumable without the lender's permission

Amortization Provides for paying a debt by installment payments; each payment covers current interest with the remainder applied to reduction of the principal

Balloon mortgage Provides for installment payments that are not enough to pay off both the principal and interest over the term of the mortgage; the final (balloon) payment to satisfy the remaining principal and interest is larger than any previous payment

Blanket mortgage Two or more parcels of real estate are pledged as security for payment of the mortgage debt

Bridge loan A short-term loan often used to finance projects until a permanent loan is obtained

Buydown The voluntary payment of discount points to reduce mortgage interest rates when the loan is made

Construction mortgage Interim, or temporary, short-term financing for creating improvements on land

Conventional loans Involves no participation by federal government agencies

Deed in lieu of foreclosure Conveyance of a property by a borrower in default to the lender to avoid record of foreclosure

Default Failure to perform an obligation, such as making mortgage payments

Defeasance clause A mortgage clause giving the borrower the right to defeat and remove the lien by paying the indebtedness in full

Deficiency judgment A court order stating that the borrower still owes a lender money when the proceeds of a foreclosure sale are not sufficient to satisfy the balance due the lender

Department of Veteran Affairs Federal agency offering a loan program that guarantees repayment of the top portion of the loan to the lender in the event the borrower defaults

Discount points Cash paid at the time of loan closing to reduce the interest rate on a loan; each point equals 1 percent of the loan amount

Equity of redemption After default and up to the time a foreclosure sale is held, the borrower has the right to redeem his property by paying the mortgage obligation; the foreclosure sale terminates the right

Federal Home Loan Mortgage Corporation (Freddie Mac) A federal agency that purchases mortgages on the secondary market to increase the availability of mortgage credit and provide greater liquidity for savings associations

Federal Housing Administration (FHA) A federal agency that insures mortgage loans to protect lending institutions; does not make mortgage loans, but protects lenders against financial loss; part of HUD

Flexible payment mortgage Mortgage plan based on the borrower's ability to pay

Foreclosure The process leading to the sale of real property pledged to secure mortgage debt

Government National Mortgage Association (Ginnie Mae) A federal agency that purchases FHA and VA mortgages on the secondary mortgage market

Grace period A specified time during which a mortgage payment may be made before the lender requires a penalty payment

Graduated payment mortgage A mortgage with lower payments in the early years of the term; payments increase at specified intervals until they are sufficient to amortize the loan over the remaining term

Home equity loan A loan against an owner's equity in his home

Hypothecating Pledging property as security for a loan

Inflation An increase in money and credit relative to available goods, resulting in higher prices

Installment land contract A means of buying land by making payments to the seller; when the property is paid for, title is transferred to the purchaser

Junior mortgage Describes any mortgage that is subordinate (lower in priority) to another mortgage

Loan-to-value ratio Compares the loan amount to the property value; expressed as a percentage

Margin For an adjustable rate mortgage, the amount above the designated index the lender adds to set the rate the borrower pays

Mortgage A two-party legal document pledging a property as security for the repayment of a loan under certain terms and conditions

Mortgagee The lender who receives the mortgage

Mortgagor The borrower who gives the mortgage

Open-end mortgage The borrower has the right to demand that the lender advance additional funds without rewriting the mortgage or incurring additional closing costs

Payment cap If the interest rate on an adjustable rate loan increases, a lender may allow a payment cap to keep the monthly payment the same, with the money for the higher interest rate being added to the principal

Predatory lending A practice in which a lender loans money to unqualified buyers.

Prepayment privilege or penalty clause A clause in a note accompanying a mortgage stating that the borrower may pay off the loan at any time without incurring a financial penalty or that a prepayment penalty will be imposed if the debt is paid off early

Promissory note or bond A note, in writing, required by a lender to provide evidence that a valid debt exists

Purchase money mortgage A mortgage given by a buyer to the seller to cover part of the purchase price or given to a third party lender to secure a loan, the proceeds of which are used to acquire the property

Rate caps With adjustable rate mortgages, limits on interest rates during the lifetime of the loan

Release clause With a blanket mortgage, allows certain parcels of property to be removed from the mortgage lien if the loan balance is reduced by a specified amount

Rural Economic and Community Development (RECD) Operates federal loan programs targeted to rural areas; makes direct loans and guarantees loans

Satisfaction of mortgage An instrument drawn by the mortgagee (lender) when the mortgage is paid in full

Secondary mortgage market Buys and sells mortgages created in the primary mortgage market; mortgages must be assignable to qualify

State of New York Mortgage Agency (SONYMA, also known as Sonny Mae) Raises money for mortgage loans from the sale of New York tax-free bonds; generally available through participating lenders at interest rates lower than most conventional loans

Straight term mortgage The borrower pays interest only for a specified term and pays the principal at the end of the term

Subprime mortgage A loan that may charge more points and have a higher interest rate than other loans; made to borrowers with lower than average credit ratings

Swing loan An interim or bridge loan usually not secured by a mortgage

Usury Laws that fix a maximum legal interest rate; the maximum rate is subject to fluctuation

Wraparound mortgage A subordinate mortgage that "wraps around" the existing first mortgage, which stays in place and is superior to the wraparound

Key Points

1. The purpose of a mortgage is to secure the payment of a debt. A mortgage creates a lien against the property.
2. If a borrower defaults on a loan, a lender may institute foreclosure proceedings. If the sale proceeds available to the lender do not satisfy the debt, the lender may sue for a deficiency judgment.

3. The borrower's rights are (a) possession of the property before default, (b) defeat of lien by paying debt in full before default, and (c) equity of redemption.

4. The lender's rights are (a) possession of the property after foreclosure, (b) foreclosure, and (c) right to assign the mortgage.

5. A buyer assuming a seller's mortgage assumes liability on the mortgage and the note. The seller remains liable on the note unless specifically released by a mortgage clause or by the lender. A buyer taking title subject to an existing mortgage has no liability on the note.

6. Conventional loans need not be insured if the loan amount does not exceed 80 percent of the property value. Most conventional insured loans are 90 percent and 95 percent loans. The insurance is called private mortgage insurance (PMI). The borrower pays the premium.

7. A fully amortized mortgage requires payments of principal and interest that will satisfy the debt over the mortgage term.

8. Various types of mortgages and loans include term, adjustable or variable rate, balloon, amortized, pledged account, graduated payment, open-end, blanket, wraparound, swing (or bridge), purchase money, construction, shared equity, home equity, reverse annuity, and package.

9. Qualified lending institutions make FHA, VA, and RHS (Rural Housing Authority) loans.

10. The FHA-insured programs include 203(b). FHA mutual mortgage insurance and the upfront mortgage insurance premium protect the lender from financial loss in the event of foreclosure. FHA establishes a maximum loan amount.

11. The Department of Veteran Affairs (VA) guarantees to the lender a maximum of 25 percent of a home loan amount up to $104,250 in the event the borrower defaults. This limits the maximum loan amount with no down payment to $417,000.

12. The primary mortgage market is the activity of lending institutions making loans directly to individual borrowers. The secondary market is the activity of lending institutions selling and buying existing mortgages. The secondary market mortgage companies include Fannie Mae (FNMA), Ginnie Mae (GNMA), and Freddie Mac (FHLMC).

13. Methods of financing include insured and uninsured conventional mortgage loans, FHA-insured loans, VA-guaranteed loans, SONYMA mortgages, RHS loans, and various types of private financing.

14. Regulation Z of the Truth in Lending Act provides for disclosure by lenders and truth in advertising.

15. Lender criteria for granting a loan include investment quality of the property, sales price and appraised value, loan-to-value ratio, types of property, and purchaser's ability to pay.

16. Income, qualifying ratios, employment history, the borrower's business organization (if any), liquid assets, monthly obligations, and credit history are considered by the lender when someone is trying to qualify for a loan.

17. Subprime mortgages are mortgages in which a lender charges a higher interest rate and high closing costs to compensate for potential losses from customers who may later default.

18. While the subprime loans have increased home ownership, they are at the center of a recent surge in mortgage defaults and foreclosures.

19. The New York Anti-Predatory Lending Law protects borrowers from lenders who charge excessive interest and points to high-risk borrowers.

Land Use Regulations

Key Terms

Abutting land Parcels of land with a common boundary

Accessory apartment An apartment not intended for commercial rental; an example is an in-law apartment in a residential home

Accessory uses Uses of a property that are incidental or subordinate to the main use of the property

Air rights Ownership right of the air space above the surface of the land; landowners may lease or sell air space to others

Area variance Permission to use land in a manner not normally allowed by the dimensional or physical requirements of the current zoning ordinance

Article 9-A Covers the sale or lease of vacant subdivided lands within and without New York only when sold through an installment land contract; covers a sale made by a salesperson, broker, owner, or any other individual empowered to sell the land

Building codes State and local rules and regulations that govern construction practices; regulate materials used in construction, electrical wiring, fire and safety standards, and sanitary equipment facilities

Building permit Local government permission to undertake construction or renovation

Census tracts Small geographical areas established by the local community and the Bureau of Census; they have numerical identification numbers

Certificate of occupancy A document permitting occupation of a structure by tenants or the owner after a satisfactory final inspection

Cluster zoning Allows a developer to place single-family houses, townhomes, apartments and other dwellings closer together in exchange for leaving parts of the development open for community enjoyment

Condemnation Actual taking of property under the power of eminent domain

Conditions Restrictions that provide for a reversion of title if they are violated

Cul-de-sacs Streets with only one outlet; dead ends

Deed restrictions In the form of covenants or conditions, they run with the land (move with the title in any subsequent conveyance) as private controls placed on real estate

Demography The study of the social and economic characteristics of a community

Density A measure of the number of families inhabiting an area of land

Doctrine of Laches If property owners do not act to enforce a restrictive covenant on a timely basis, the court will not apply the restriction against the violator and the covenant will be terminated; if landowners are lax in protecting their rights, they may lose them

Eminent domain The right or power of government and its agencies to take private property for public use; must be for the public good

Environmental impact statement The process that describes and analyzes a proposed action that may have a significant effect on the environment

Escheat The power of the state to take title to a deceased person's property when no one else is qualified to receive the title

Family According to New York law, any of the following: a group of up to three people who are not married, blood relatives, or adopted living together as a single housekeeping unit; an individual or two or more persons related by blood or marriage or adoption living together in one dwelling; one or more persons living as a single housekeeping unit, as distinguished from a group occupying a hotel, club fraternity, or sorority house

Group home A residential facility for five or more adults who have been institutionalized for various reasons and then released

Home occupation Use of residential property by an owner or lessee for a small business; may be conducted only by the residents of the dwelling and must be incidental and secondary to the use of the dwelling

Infrastructure Support systems of a community such as water, wastewater treatment, utilities, schools, roadways, medical services, police, and fire departments

Lead agency The agency that oversees the environmental assessment process and makes the final decisions

Moratorium Imposed by a municipality, it is a delay in allowing property development in the municipality

New York State Office of Parks, Recreation and Historic Preservation Administers federal and state preservation programs authorized by federal law and by the New York Historic Preservation Law

Nonconforming use ("grandfathered in") A preexisting use of property different from that specified by the current zoning code

Police power Enables government to fulfill its responsibility to provide for the public health, safety, and welfare

Setback Specified distances from the front property line and from the interior property lines to the building line

Special use permit A use not permitted in the zone except with the special permission of the planning board or other legislative body

Spot zoning Rezoning of a specific property to permit a use different from the zoning requirements for that area; illegal in New York

Subdivision Land that is divided into lots for development purposes

Survey The measurements of the boundaries and the total physical dimensions of the property

Taking The act of a government body obtaining a property under its power of eminent domain

Topography The physical features and contours of the land

Transfer of development rights Purchase of the development rights of another property, such as those of a historic property that cannot make use of them

Use variance Permission to use the land for a purpose prohibited under current zoning restrictions

Variance A permitted deviation from zoning ordinance requirements

Key Points

1. Individual owners have the right to place private controls on their own real estate. The purpose of a deed restriction is to limit the use or appearance of a property.

2. In New York, the State Environmental Quality Review Act (SEQRA) controls environmental impacts. An environmental impact statement (EIS) evaluates the effect the environment has on the property.

3. Public land use controls include police power, taxation, eminent domain, and escheat.

4. The Interstate Land Sales Full Disclosure Act regulates the sale of unimproved lots in interstate commerce to prevent fraudulent schemes in selling land sight unseen.

5. New York Article 9-A protects state residents in the purchase or lease of vacant subdivided lands in and outside of New York purchased through installment land contracts.

6. The New York State Uniform Fire Prevention and Building Code provides minimum standards for all types of buildings.

7. The New York building code requires that a property owner obtain a building permit from the appropriate local government authority (usually the building department) before constructing or renovating a commercial building or residential property.

8. Eminent domain is the right of government to take private land for public use.

9. If an individual dies without a will and there are no heirs or creditors, his property reverts to the state through the power of escheat.

10. Types of zones include residential, commercial, industrial, vacant land, agricultural, public open space, parklands, recreation areas, and institutional.

11. In New York, local planning boards oversee the type of land use within the municipality and have the authority to review site plans.

12. Density is the occupancy restriction for the number of families that can inhabit a certain plot of land. The purpose of planning board rules governing density is to avoid overcrowding residential areas.

13. A use or an area variance is a permitted deviation from specific requirements of a zoning ordinance.

14. With spot zoning, a specific property within a zoned area is rezoned to permit a use different from the zoning requirements for that zoned area. Spot zoning is illegal in New York.

15. A use or an area variance is a permitted deviation from specific requirements of a zoning ordinance.

16. A nonconforming use occurs when a preexisting use of property in a zoned area is different from that specified by the zoning code. This is a preexisting nonconforming use, or a "grandfathered" use.

Construction and Environmental Issues
Part I Construction

Key Terms

Amperage The amount of electricity flowing though a wire

Balloon framing An alternative to platform framing; uses wall studs that run from the foundation through the first and second floors to the ceiling support; rarely used in residential construction

Bearing walls Walls, including the outside wall frame, that support the ceiling and/or the roof

British Thermal Unit (BTU) A measure of heat energy; the amount of heat required to raise the temperature of one pound of water by one degree Fahrenheit

Building plan A detailed architectural rendering of a structure; blueprint

Building specifications Written narratives that describe the building plan and materials

Circuit breakers Devices that that switch off electrical power for a given circuit if the current increases beyond the capacity of the system

Distribution panel Metal box containing electrical circuit breakers or fuses; where outside power enters a structure to be distributed inside

Double top plate Also known as a flitch beam, used to tie walls together and provide support for the ceiling and roof system

Eave The lowest part of the roof which project beyond the walls of the structure

Fascia The material facing the outer edge of the soffit; if guttering is installed on a roof, it is fastened to the fascia

Flashing Metallic material used in certain areas of the roof to prevent water from seeping into the structure

Footing The most important foundation building block; the concrete base below the frost line that supports a structure's foundation

Foundation walls Generally composed of poured concrete, masonry block, or sometimes brick; the height of the foundation wall determines whether the structure will have a full basement or a crawl space

Frieze board A component of the roof overhang fastened directly under the soffit against the top of the wall; both decorative and functional

Fuse A device that melts to open a circuit and cut off electrical power when overheating occurs

Girder A main carrying beam, either a steel beam or several wooden members fastened together, that spans the distance from one side of a foundation to the other

Headers Also known as lintels; framing members that reinforce door and window openings

Joists Framing members used for floor and ceiling framing

Lally columns Support the main carrying beam of the structure; round steel columns filled with concrete that rest on a base plate, which is the column-footing pad

National Electric Code A national standard for electrical installation and service written to safeguard people and property from hazards arising from the use of electricity

Pitch Slope of the roof

Platform framing Framing in which the structure rests on a subfloor platform; the most common type of framing for residential construction

Post-and-beam framing Framing in which studs are much larger than ordinary studs (they may be four or six inches square); the larger posts are placed several feet apart; seldom used in residential construction

R-factor The degree of a wall's resistance to heat transfer; used to rate insulation: the larger the R-factor, the greater the degree of insulation

Rafters Long wood members fastened to the ends of the ceiling joists to form roof gables

Ridge beam The highest part of the framing; forms the apex, or top line, of the roof

Septic system A household wastewater treatment system consisting of a house sewer, septic tank, distribution box, and absorption field or seepage pit

Sheathing A plywood covering placed over exterior framing members; sheetrock or wallboard may be used

Sill plate The first wooden member of a structure; used as the nailing surface for the floor system

Slab-on-grade construction A concrete slab used instead of a foundation wall; the slab is poured directly on the ground, eliminating the crawl space or basement

Soffit The area under the roof extension; made of wood, aluminum, or vinyl

Sole plate A horizontal base plate that serves as the foundation for the wall system

Studs Wood framing members are lumber with a nominal dimension of 2 inches thickness
Urea Formaldehyde Foam Insulation (UFFI) Widely used in homes from 1970s to the 1980s; a hot, viscous mixture sprayed inside the sheathing where it solidifies

Voltage The electrical pressure that pushes through a wire

Key Points

1. In New York, residential and commercial structures must comply with state and local building codes. The New York Uniform Fire Prevention and Building Code supplies the minimum requirements. The New York Energy Code governs types of insulation and energy efficiencies.
2. New York has laws and regulations that govern on-site well regulations and on-site sanitary waste systems.
3. The sanitary waste system or drainage system of a structure carries wastewater and used water from the structure and deposits it in the public sewer system or private wastewater treatment system.
4. Other site considerations in the planning stage include drainage, landscaping, shading, and walkways.
5. Footings support the foundation wall and, therefore, the entire weight of the structure.
6. Foundation walls may be poured concrete, masonry block, or sometimes brick. The height of the foundation wall determines whether the structure has a crawl space or a full basement.

7. Framing is the wooden skeleton of a structure. Framing members are lumber with a nominal dimension of 2 inches thick.

8. The floor system starts with the sill plate nailed to the foundation system. Wood joists support the subfloor material.

9. Wall framing is usually 2" x 4" studs placed 16 inches on center. The most common wall-framing system is the platform method. Alternative methods are balloon and post-and-beam framing.

10. The roof structural skeleton is usually built with 2" x 8" ceiling joists and 2"-x 6" or 2" x 8" rafters.

11. The main purpose of insulation is to resist the flow of heat from one area to another. Insulation is rated on an R-factor; the larger the R-factor, the greater the degree of insulation.

12. HVAC stands for heating, ventilation, and air conditioning. Some systems use fuel oil or natural gas for energy, while others use electricity.

13. Heating systems found in the home are usually hot water, steam, forced warm air, or electric. The heat pump is another type of heating system.

14. Forced-air heating and cooling systems use a central fan or blower to distribute the heated or cooled air throughout the structure. Hot water heating systems use circulator pumps to propel the heated water through pipes to the convectors.

15. Air conditioning units are placed inside or outside a structure. Components of an air conditioner include liquid refrigerant, an evaporator, a compressor, and a condenser.

16. The plumbing system consists of two systems: the water supply system for drinking, cooking, and washing and the drainage system for wastewater.

17. Hot water systems commonly found in residential construction include gas and electric water tanks as well as other types of systems that are connected to the heat source.

18. Electric power is brought to a structure through outside cables and is delivered through conductors (wires) to the building wiring system.

19. The New York General Business Law provides for a one-year builder's warranty against construction defects and a six-year warranty against material defects.

20. In New York, every one- and two-family dwelling as well as apartments in multiple dwellings, including residential condominiums and cooperatives, must have an installed operable single-station smoke detector.

21. New York regulations require that at least one functioning carbon monoxide detector be installed near the bedroom(s) in all one- and two-family properties, including condominiums and cooperatives, that are constructed or offered for sale. When a property is transferred, a smoke alarm and carbon monoxide detector affidavit is required.

Construction and Environmental Issues

Part II Environmental Issues

Key Terms

Asbestos A fibrous mineral found in rocks and soil throughout the world; used in construction because it is strong, durable, fire retardant, and an efficient insulator; improper handling of asbestos products results in lung disease

Chlordane A chemical insecticide and termiticide banned in the early 1980s because of its toxicity

Chloro-fluoro-carbons (CFCs) Manmade chemical substances used in hundreds of applications, including refrigerators and air conditioners, styrofoam products, aerosol dispensers, and cleanings agents; a danger to the ozone layer

Clean Air Act (1972) A comprehensive federal law intended to control air pollution; a 1990 amendment bans the release of CFCs and HCFCs during the service, maintenance, and disposal of air conditioners and other equipment that uses these refrigerants

Comprehensive Environmental Response, Compensation and Liability Act (CERCLA)(1980) A federal law enacted to correct environmental problems created by uncontrolled waste disposal

Due diligence Because liability for environmental problems passes to new owners in the sale of large tracts of land or commercial property, lenders, purchasers, and tenants often conduct environmental reviews of the property

Electromagnetic fields Magnetic fields created by electricity flowing through a wire
Friable Flaky or crumbly texture of asbestos when hand pressure is applied

Hydro-chloro-fluoro-carbons (HCFCs) Also known as Freon, a non toxic chemical substance used in most home air-conditioning units; when released poses a danger to the ozone layer

Kilovolt A measure of voltage flowing through a power line

Lead A metallic element found worldwide in rocks and soils; can be present in drinking water, house paint, dust, and soil around a home; toxic

PCB A manmade, odorless, liquid organic compound; PCBs are used to cool and insulate electrical transformers; known to appear in ground water and soil; a carcinogen
Radon A colorless, odorless, tasteless, radioactive gas present in soil and well water; enters homes through openings such as cracks in concrete, floor drains, sump pump openings, wall/floor joints in basements, and the pores in hollow block walls

Sick building syndrome Occurs when many people in a commercial building fall ill with a variety of complaints ranging from allergic reactions to flu-like symptoms to more serious complaints; may be blamed on poor air quality inside the building

State Environmental Quality Review Act (SEQRA) (1976) Calls for the preparation of an environmental impact statement on any actions that may affect the environment; this action may be proposed by a governmental body, private individuals, or entities whose projects require governmental approval

Superfund Amendments and Reauthorization Act (SARA) (1986) An amendment to CERCLA imposing stringent clean-up standards and expanding the definition of persons liable for clean-up costs

Wetlands Marshes, swamps, bogs which are protected areas as they provide flood and storm water control, surface and groundwater protection, erosion control, pollution treatment, fish and wildlife habitats and natural beauty

Key Points

1. Long-standing environmental issues relative to real estate include drinking water, wastewater treatment, and pest infestation. Contemporary issues include the use of chemical contaminants such as asbestos, lead, radon, and PCBs. Other present and future concerns include underground storage tanks, electromagnetic fields, mold, and the release of chlorofluorocarbons.

2. Federal and state legislation provide regulations and guidelines for environmental policy.

3. The federal Safe Drinking Water Act is New York's guideline for drinking water regulations. The New York Department of Health oversees the safety of drinking water in New York and the installation and approval of individual on-site wastewater treatment facilities of less than 1,000 gallons per residence.

4. Federal law mandates that in the sale or lease of pre-1978 residential properties, sellers or their agents must distribute a lead hazard pamphlet and disclose any known information to the buyers or their agent concerning lead paint. The parties must agree to a ten-day period for a lead paint assessment to take place before a purchaser becomes obligated under the contract. Sales and lease contracts must include specific disclosure and acknowledgment language.

5. Asbestos, a carcinogen, is in many building products that have numerous applications within the building industry.

6. Lead can be present in drinking water, in interior and exterior paint, and in dust and soil in and around a home.

7. The New York State Department of Environmental Conservation (NYSDEC) oversees and protects wetlands. Construction can take place on or near a wetland. Builders must obtain approval for regulated activities from the state through local and federal governments.

8. Radon from surrounding soil enters a home through small spaces and openings. The only way to detect radon is to test for it.

9. The Clean Air Act gives the EPA the power to regulate air pollution, identify air-polluting substances, and mandate the states to implement protective measures.

10. One source of air pollution in the home may be urea-formaldehyde foam insulation (UFFI), which contains large amounts of formaldehyde.

11. Another source of home air pollution is insecticides. Chlordane is a chemical insecticide and termiticide banned since the early 1980s.

12. Bacteria are a source of air pollution in homes and buildings. Sometimes large numbers of people in a commercial building fall ill from a chemical illness called sick building syndrome.

13. A PCB is a toxic, synthetic liquid organic compound. Some of New York's soils and waterways may contain PCBs.

14. The State Environmental Quality Review (SEQR) is a process that requires all levels of government to assess the environmental significance of actions that they have discretion to review, approve, fund, or undertake.

15. An environmental impact statement (EIS) describes and analyzes a proposed action that may have a significant effect on the environment.

16. Because of liability for environmental cleanup, lenders, purchasers, and tenants often conduct due diligence reviews of property before transfer.

17. The NYSDEC regulates the bulk storage of chemicals and petroleum both aboveground and underground. These tanks are monitored for leakage.

18. Electromagnetic fields are present where there are power lines. New York has adopted a prudent avoidance policy.

19. Chlorofluorocarbons are synthetic chemical substances used in refrigerators and air conditioners. The release of these chemicals threatens the ozone layer.

Valuation Process and Pricing Properties

Key Terms

Appraisal An unbiased estimate of the nature, quality, value, or utility of an interest in or aspect of identified real estate and related personalty, based on factual data; it is an opinion of the market value of a property, as of a given date, supported in writing with collected data and logical reasoning

Comparative market analysis (CMA) An analysis of the competition that a property offered for sale will face in the marketplace; not an appraisal

Cost The total expenditure for labor, materials, legal services, architectural design, financing, taxes during construction, interest, contractor's overhead and profit, and entrepreneurial overhead and profit

Cost Approach Appraisal method for evaluating properties that have few, if any, comparables and are not income producing

Depreciation Loss in value from any cause

Direct costs Also called hard costs, they include the cost of labor and materials

Evaluation The study of the nature, quality, or utility of certain property interests in which a value estimate is not necessarily required; examples are studies of land utilization, highest and best use, marketability, feasibility, and supply and demand

External Obsolescence Changes in surrounding land use patterns resulting in increased traffic, air pollution, and other hazards and nuisances

Functional Obsolescence Flawed or faulty property rendered inferior because of advances and change in such items as wiring, equipment or design

Highest and best use The use of land that will preserve its usefulness, provide the greatest income, and result in the highest land value

Income Approach Appraisal method used to estimate the present value of properties that produce income

Indirect costs The costs that create and support the project include architectural and engineering fees, professional fees such as surveyors, attorneys, and appraisers, financing costs, administrative costs, lease-up costs and filing fees

Insured value The cost of replacing or reproducing a structure in the event of a total loss due to an insured hazard

Investment value Value based on the amount of financial return that a property would produce

Market value The most probable price, as of a specific date, in cash, or in terms equivalent to cash, or in other precisely revealed terms, at which the specified property rights should sell after reasonable exposure in a competitive market, under all conditions requisite to a fair sale, with the buyer and seller each acting prudently, knowledgeably, and for self interest, and assuming that neither is under duress

Mortgage value Value based on what a lender believes the property will bring at a foreclosure sale or subsequent resale

Plottage Small plots of land are combined to form a larger plot

Price The amount a purchaser agrees to pay and a seller agrees to accept under the circumstances surrounding the transaction

Residential market analysis A careful study of the individual property being listed as it stands on its own and in light of current market conditions

Sales comparison approach Primary appraisal method for estimating the value of single-family, owner-occupied dwellings and vacant land

Valuation Establishes an opinion of value utilizing a totally objective approach; it is the process of estimating the value of an identified interest in a specific property as of a given date

Value in use Property considered more for its value to the owner and not for its value if placed on the market

Key Points

1. An appraisal is an estimate of value based on factual data as of a specific date for a particular purpose on a specified property.
2. Valuation is the process of estimating the value of an identified interest in a specific property as of a given date. Besides market value, other types of value include value in use, insurance value, investment value, assessed value, and mortgage loan value.
3. Market value is the amount of money a typical buyer will give in exchange for a property.
4. Evaluation, as compared with valuation, is a study of the quality or utility of a property without reference to a specific estimate of value.
5. Various evaluation studies include marketability, feasibility, supply and demand, land utilization, and highest and best use. In the context of market value, highest and best use is the most probable use. It may or may not be the present use of the property.
6. Price is the amount a purchaser agrees to pay and a seller agrees to accept under the circumstances surrounding the transaction.
7. Cost is composed of a number of factors that equal the total dollar expenditure to construct the improvements. Included are direct costs, such as labor and materials, and indirect costs, such as professional fees, filing fees, and other items in the construction process.
8. A comparative market analysis (CMA) is an analysis of the competition in the marketplace that a property will face upon sale attempts.
9. A residential market analysis consists of a study of recently sold properties, currently competing properties, recently expired properties, buyer appeal, market position, assets and drawbacks, area market conditions, recommended terms, and price range.
10. The degree of competence, diligence, documentation, and effective communication skills on the part of the licensee is integral to effective marketing of the property.
11. Highest and best use refers to the use of land aimed at preserving its usefulness, providing the greatest income, and resulting in the highest land value. To achieve the highest and best use, land is improved using capital and labor to make the land productive.
12. A first step in site valuation is to conduct a feasibility study. Factors reviewed are the cost of site development (including environmental factors), costs of financing (including prevailing interest

rates), tax considerations, rates of return on similar types of investments, and the benefit to and acceptance by the community.

13. A site is generally valued using the sales comparison approach.

14. Appraisals commonly use three approaches to value: the sales comparison approach, the cost approach, and the income approach. The sales comparison approach most closely resembles the comparative market analysis.

15. Part of the listing process involves recommending to the owner a market price that will be the listing price.

16. A comparison of the property with similar properties that have sold recently (within the last six months), other properties currently listed for sale, and evaluation of expired listings determines the price.

Human Rights and Fair Housing

Key Terms

Americans with Disabilities Act (1992) Protects the rights of individuals with disabilities with regard to access to commercial facilities, public accommodations, and new housing developments with at least four units

Blockbusting Occurs when real estate salespersons induce owners to list property for sale or rent by telling them that persons of a particular race, color, national origin, sex, religion, disability, or familial status are moving into the area; also when real estate firms sell a home in a neighborhood to a person from one of the protected classes with the sole intent to cause property owners to panic and place their property for sale at reduced prices

Cease and desist zone Established by the DOS after determining that some homeowners within certain geographic areas have been subject to intense and repeated solicitation by real estate agents; upon establishment of a cease and desist zone, homeowners in the zone may be placed on a list indicating that they do not desire to sell, lease, or list their residential property or be solicited by real estate agents

Civil Rights Act of 1866 The first significant statute affecting equal housing opportunity; it is interpreted to prohibit all racial discrimination

Department of Housing and Urban Development (HUD) A federal regulatory agency through which civil rights violations can be reported

Disability Legally defined as a physical or mental impairment that greatly limits one or more of a person's major life activities

The Fair Housing Amendments Act of 1988 Prohibits discrimination based on mental or physical handicap or familial status

Fair Housing poster A poster that an amendment to the Fair Housing Act of 1968 requires to be prominently displayed in real estate brokerage offices

Familial status Legally defined as an adult with children under 18, a person who is pregnant, or one who has legal custody of a child or who is in the process of obtaining custody

Federal Fair Housing Act (Civil Rights Act of 1968) Prohibits discrimination in housing on the basis of race, color, religion, or national origin

Filtering down Properties in neighborhoods that were once middle or upper income decline in value, allowing people with lower incomes to purchase them

Housing and Community Development Act of 1974 Federal law prohibiting discrimination based on gender

Human Rights Law Also known as Article 15 of the Executive Law, prohibits discrimination in the rental and leasing of housing, land, commercial space, and other non–real estate related activities

Jones v. Alfred H. Mayer Co., The U.S. Supreme Court applied the older Civil Rights Act of 1866 to prohibit any racially based discrimination in housing. This court ruling is important because the Federal Fair Housing Act provides exemptions under certain circumstances. Because of the court's determination in Jones v. Mayer, exemptions in the Fair Housing Act cannot be used to allow racial discrimination under any circumstances

Marital status Individuals who are either married or single

Multiple dwellings Residences that contain three or more family units

Nonsolicitation order An order from DOS prohibiting licensees from soliciting listings for the sale or purchase of real property in certain areas of the state

Redlining Term applied to lending institutions' refusing to make loans to purchase, construct, or repair dwellings by discriminating on the basis of race, color, religion, sex, national origin, handicap or familial status

Steering Illegal practice of directing prospective minority purchasers to presently integrated areas to avoid integration of nonintegrated areas

Testers Volunteers or employees of federal and state agencies as well as private civil rights groups who visit real estate offices posing as prospective home seekers to see if race influences the information or services provided

Key Points

1. The Civil Rights Act of 1968, known as the Fair Housing Act, prohibits discrimination in housing because of race, color, religion, sex, national origin, age, handicap, or familial status.
2. Discrimination is prohibited in the (a) sale or rental of housing, (b) advertising of the sale or rental of housing, (c) financing of housing, and (d) provision of real estate brokerage services. The act forbids blockbusting.
3. The Federal Fair Housing Act has certain exemptions, but New York laws that are more restrictive preempt these exemptions.
4. The Civil Rights Act of 1964 prohibited discrimination in any housing program receiving federal money but did not cover privately financed housing.
5. The Civil Rights Act of 1866 prohibits discrimination based only on race. The prohibition is not limited to housing, but includes real estate transactions. The act may be enforced only by civil suit in federal court. This law has no exemptions.
6. Supreme Court decisions such as *Plessy v. Ferguson* (1896), separate but equal; *Buchanan v. Warley* (1917), disallowing block-by-block segregation; and *Brown v. Board of Education* (1954), separate but unequal shaped much of U.S. policy.

7. Enforcement of Title VIII of the 1968 Civil Rights Act was amended in 1988. Enforcement procedures include (a) administrative procedure through the Office of Equal Opportunity of HUD that attempts voluntary conciliation and then can refer the case to an administrative law judge, who can impose financial penalties of $10,000 to $50,000; (b) civil suit in federal court; and (c) action by the U. S. Attorney General, who may file a suit in federal court and impose penalties of up to $50,000 on the first offense in a "pattern of discrimination."

8. The Americans with Disabilities Act provides that individuals with disabilities cannot be denied access to public transportation or any commercial facility or public accommodation. Barriers in existing buildings must be removed if readily achievable. New buildings must be readily accessible and usable by individuals with disabilities.

9. New York is governed by Article 15 of the Executive Law, called the Human Rights Law. This law adds four protected classes not included in federal law—marital status, age, sexual orientation, and military status. It covers the lease and sale of commercial space and land as well as residential housing.

10. The antidiscrimination agency in New York is the Division of Human Rights (DHR.). Complaints must be filed with the Division within one year of an alleged discriminatory act.

11. The New York City Commission on Human Rights is the enforcement agency for antidiscrimination policy in the five boroughs that compose New York City. New York City law includes three more protected classes to those covered by New York State law: citizenship or alienage, lawful occupation, and partnership status.

Real Estate Mathematics

Key Terms

Acre 43,560 square feet

Commission A percentage of the sales price

Front foot A linear foot of property frontage on a street or highway

Gross Income Income received without subtracting expenses

Income The amount of money one receives

Interest Calculated by multiplying the rate as a percentage times the principal balance

Net Operating Income Gross income less operating expenses

Point Fee charged by a lender equal to 1% of the loan amount

Rate A percentage

Tax Rate Determined by the amount of the tax levy and expressed either in dollars per $100 of assessed value or in mills,(one mill is one-tenth of a cent) per $1,000 of assessed value

Value The total amount of worth or cost of the unit

Key Points

1. In the real estate business, many calculations involve percentages which is a number divided by 100.

2. An increase in property value is known as appreciation; a decrease in value is known as depreciation.

3. A hectare is equal to 2.47 acres

4. The perimeter is the entire outer boundary of a figure such as a plot of land or the measure around a figure, such as a house or building.

5. Debt service is the annual amount to be paid to retire or regularly reduce a loan or mortgage balance.

6. Many mortgages are paid through a type of installment plan each month known as amortization.

7. A balloon mortgage provides for installment payments that are not enough to pay off the principal and interest over the term of the mortgage. A balloon mortgage is also known as a partially amortized mortgage because the loan does not amortize out at the due date.

8. Prorations at closing involve the division between the seller and the buyer of annual real property taxes, rents, homeowner's association dues, and other items that may have been paid or must be paid.

9. Profit or loss is always based upon the amount of money invested in the property.

10. The capitalization rate is the percentage of the investment the owner will receive back each year from the net income from the property. The rate is based upon the dollar invested and the annual net income from the property.

Municipal Agencies

Key Terms

Architectural review boards Composed mostly of people with expertise in art, architecture, and planning, oversees building design

Building department Enforces the building code; protects the public by ensuring that code restrictions are followed

Conservation Advisory Council Advises in the development, management, and protection of the municipality's natural resources

County health department Cooperates with the NYS Department of Health; these local agencies may have laws that are more restrictive than state law

Historic Preservation/Landmark Commission Identifies and protects historic landmarks

Planning boards On all government levels, plans for the future of the region; the boards consider the available natural and supplied resources of the community

Receiver of taxes The collecting officer for each city and town who receives real property taxes and assessments during a specified collection period

Tax assessor An elected or appointed local official or officials who have the legal authority to independently estimate the value of real property in an assessing unit

Village board of trustees The governing body of villages

Zoning board of appeals Reviews administrative rulings made by the planning board or other legislative body, grants or denies exceptions and special permits, and processes applications for variances

Key Points

1. The city charter and town or village ordinance; the county, city, town, and village handbooks, information officers, and websites are sources of information regarding the agencies within a municipality.
2. A legislative body creates an administrative government agency. These agencies are empowered by the state legislature as well as by the legislative bodies of cities, counties, towns, and villages.
3. The legislative power of a city is vested in its city council or common council. The town council or board is the governing body of towns. The village board of trustees is the governing body of villages. All members of these government bodies are elected.
4. Planning boards on all government levels plan for the future of the region, considering the available natural and supplied resources of the community. Planning boards work with the master plan of the municipality or region.
5. The zoning board of appeals decides on the granting of variances for the municipality. The board is an interpreter of the zoning ordinance.
6. The local legislative body of any city, town, or village can appoint a conservation advisory council to advise in the development, management, and protection of its natural resources. The council can conduct research regarding environment projects.
7. The New York regulatory agency that oversees wetlands is the Department of Environmental Conservation. Under New York law, local governments also can manage wetlands. The Conservation Advisory Council and/or the Wetlands Commissions perform local management.
8. The Historic Preservation/Landmark Commissions in cities, towns, villages, and counties regulate special conditions and restrictions for the protection of places and objects that have a special character, historical, or aesthetic interest.
9. Building departments enforce the building code. This department provides building permits and certificates of occupancy. Building inspectors visit construction sites to ensure that construction complies with all applicable building codes.
10. The tax assessor is a local government official who estimates the value of real property within a city, town, or village's boundaries. All properties are assessed at a uniform percentage of value. The tax assessor maintains tax maps and tax records for the municipality.
11. The city or town engineer estimates the costs of paving, sewers, and sidewalks, and other public works projects. He supervises streets and other public works activities.
12. County departments of health oversee drinking water safety, including standards for private and community well construction and well water safety and regulation, septic system approval, and certain wastewater treatment approval.

Property Insurance

Key Terms

Actual cash value (ACV) A type of insurance in which the insured is reimbursed for the replacement cost minus the physical depreciation of the lost or damaged property

Deductible The amount the insured must pay toward a claim before receiving any policy benefits

Liability insurance Insurance coverage to protect against claims alleging that one's negligence or inappropriate action resulted in bodily injury or property damage

Package policy A policy that includes several different types of coverage, such as property insurance and liability insurance

Property insurance Protects a home or income/business property against any physical damage or loss of assets in the case of fire, theft, or vandalism

Replacement cost A type of insurance in which the insured is covered and reimbursed for the actual cost of replacing the damaged property

Umbrella policy An excess liability policy that provides additional coverage above that offered by primary policies

Key Points

1. Property insurance protects a home, a business, or income property against any physical damage or loss of assets in the case of fire, theft, or vandalism. The typical homeowner's policy has two main sections: Section I covers the property of the insured; Section II provides personal liability coverage to the insured.

2. Liability insurance is insurance coverage to protect against claims alleging that one's negligence or inappropriate action resulted in bodily injury or property damage.

3. A package policy includes several different types of coverage, such as property insurance and liability insurance.

5. The actual cash value (ACV) basis for a policy means that the insured is reimbursed for the replacement cost minus the physical depreciation of the lost or damaged property.

6. Replacement cost means that the insured is covered and reimbursed for the actual cost of replacing the damaged property.

7. Generally, if the insured purchases coverage on a replacement cost basis and insures the home for at least 80 percent of its replacement cost, the insurance is automatically issued on a replacement cost basis.

8. The New York Property Insurance Underwriting Association (NYPIUA) is a pool of all insurance companies writing fire insurance in New York. It offers fire and extended coverage as well as coverage for vandalism, malicious mischief, and sprinkler leakage to consumers who are unable to purchase this type of insurance from individual insurance companies.

9. The Federal Emergency Management Association (FEMA) administers the National Flood Insurance Program. Insurance coverage for losses resulting from floods is generally not provided in any homeowners or tenants policies.

10. Section 3445 of the Insurance Law requires that insurers provide proper disclosure to their insured's of any windstorm deductibles attached to their homeowner's policies.

11. Under New York law, an insurance company may cancel a homeowners or tenants policy by issuing a cancellation notice during the first 60 days it is in effect as long as the cancellation notice states the specific reason or reasons for the cancellation.

12. Specific insurance is available for rental/income property. Commercial General Liability (GCL) insurance is a basic business liability policy that covers four forms of injury: bodily injury that results in actual physical damage or loss, property damage that results in actual physical damage or loss, personal injury, and advertising injury.

13. An umbrella policy is an excess liability policy that provides additional coverage above that offered by primary policies.

14. Real estate agents should counsel their buyers as to the importance of obtaining property insurance, lender requirements, and the escrow account for property insurance premiums.

Taxes and Assessments

Key Terms

Ad valorem Latin for according to value; in New York, the real property tax is based on the fair market value of real property

Apportionment Division of property and school tax monies so that school districts, counties, towns and cities in the different municipalities all pay their fair share of the tax levy

Appropriation Occurs when a government agency sets aside funds for a certain purpose.

Approved assessing unit One that has completed a property reevaluation and is certified by the New York State Office of Real Property Services (NYSORPS)

Assessed value The value of a property as determined by a tax assessor

Assessing units Counties, cities, towns, villages, school districts, and special districts that raise money through real property taxes

Assessment A percentage of a property's market value; this figure is used for property tax purposes and ultimately determines how the total tax is shared among property owners

Assessment roll Usually in section, block/lot order, it lists all real property in the taxing jurisdiction, with information about each parcel, including its assessed value and exempt status

Board of Assessment Review (BAR) An appointed body consisting of three to five members that hears and decides upon grievances from taxpayers

Equalization rate Represents the average percentage of market value at which a municipality's assessment is set

Exemptions Full exemptions or partial reductions in property taxes available to certain people, institutions, and organizations

Grievance A written complaint filed with the local board of assessment review protesting a property tax assessment

Homestead Properties that are completely or partially used as the owner's residence and are classified as such for tax purposes

Non-homestead All properties not classified as homesteads; includes commercial, industrial, special franchise, utility properties, and some vacant land

Residential assessment ratios (RARs) Used by assessors as a general measure of assessment equity; also used by taxpayers in board of assessment review grievances and/or small claims hearings.

Special assessment A tax levied by the taxing unit to collect payment for a share of the cost of improvements made to areas nearby or adjoining the property; constitutes a specific lien against the property until paid

Special assessment districts Localities that raise money through real property taxes

***Tax certiorari* proceeding** A New York Supreme Court review of cases requested by taxpayers who protest their assessment and are still dissatisfied with the decision of the board of assessment review

Tax exemptions Taxing authorities may grant full or partial exemptions from tax obligations to certain groups

Tax levy The amount that a municipality must raise to meet budgetary requirements by taxing real property

Tax lien An encumbrance against a property filed by the taxing jurisdiction for delinquency in paying real property taxes

Tax rate The amount of money needed by a municipality to meet budgetary requirements divided by the taxable assessed and nonexempt value of all the real property within that jurisdiction

Taxable status date The ownership and physical condition of real property are assessed according to price fixed as of the valuation date; all applications must be filed with the assessor by this date

Uniform percentage Each assessing unit sets the percentage of market value to be used as the assessment standard and must apply this percentage uniformly to all properties within its boundaries

Key Points

1. In New York, property is taxed on an ad valorem basis, that is, according to the market value of the property.
2. A tax bill is determined by a formula that includes two items: the property's assessment and the tax rate of the taxing jurisdiction.
3. A property's assessment is a percentage of its market value and, in most areas outside of New York City and Nassau County, must be a uniform percentage of the property's market value throughout the taxing jurisdiction.
4. All property is subject to assessment; however, not all property is taxed. Property tax exemptions may be full or partial.
5. An approved assessing unit is a taxing jurisdiction that has completed a property reevaluation and is certified by the New York State Office of Real Property Services.

6. The assessment roll that describes all properties and their assessed value is published each year. Taxpayers who disagree with their assessment may file a complaint called a grievance.

7. If taxpayers are still dissatisfied with the decision of the board of assessment review, they may file a complaint with the New York Supreme Court, called a tax certiorari proceeding, or be heard by specially appointed small claims hearing officers.

8. The tax rate must be sufficient to provide the amount of revenue to accomplish the budgetary requirements of the local governmental unit.

9. The equalization rate represents the average percentage of market value at which assessments in a municipality are set at a given point in time.

10. If a property owner is delinquent in paying property taxes, his taxing jurisdiction may impose a lien against the property.

Condominiums and Cooperatives

Key Terms

Alteration agreement Describes the terms under which the cooperative gives permission to a shareholder before making any changes or improvements to the unit the shareholder occupies

Board package Documents of a proposed purchaser reviewed by a cooperative board

Bylaws The shareholder's rights and obligations for a condominium

Common Elements Ownership of areas and utilities in a condominium or cooperative building shared by owners

Condominium A form of ownership of real property that consists of individual ownership of some aspects and co-ownership in other aspects of the property

Condop A building that includes condominium and cooperative ownership in the same structure

Cooperative A form of ownership in which stockholders in a corporation occupy property owned by the corporation under a lease

Covenants, conditions, and restrictions (CCRs) In a condominium, the document that sets forth all of the rights, duties, and obligations of the unit owners

Declaration A master deed containing a legal description of the condominium facility, a plat of the property, plans and specifications for the building and units, a description of the common areas, and the degree of ownership in the common areas available to each owner

Flip tax Sometimes imposed by the board of directors of a cooperative; this is a revenue-producing device for the cooperative corporation; usually paid by the seller at closing

Flipping Investors buy a property at a certain price, then immediately sell the property at a higher price.

House rules Rules in a cooperative that cover issues as garbage disposal, maintenance, noise, and conflict resolution.

Letter of intent An agreement to purchase a condominium; may or may not be binding

Maintenance Monthly payment by shareholder to the cooperative corporation

Offering plan or statement The document filed with the New York Attorney General detailing the setup and rules for a condominium or cooperative

Proprietary lease A lease in a cooperative apartment
Recognition agreement Describes the relationship between the cooperative and other entities

Share loan A type of loan in which stock is the collateral; used for cooperative purchases

Sponsor The developer of a condominium or cooperative

Key Points

1. The main difference between cooperatives and condominiums is the form of ownership. With a cooperative, a cooperative corporation usually owns the land, buildings, and property rights and all interests in the corporation.
2. The purchaser of a cooperative becomes a shareholder of the corporation and a tenant in the building. The tenant-shareholder has the right of occupancy. A cooperative purchaser does not obtain a deed; instead, he receives a proprietary lease issued by the cooperative corporation.
3. A financial statement should include a balance sheet describing assets and liabilities, an income and expense statement (statement of operations), and a cash flow statement. For a cooperative, the status of the underlying mortgage is very important.
4. Cooperative ownership documents typically include the articles of incorporation, bylaws, proprietary lease or occupancy agreement, subscription agreement, and house rules.
5. The developer that constructs or converts a building into a cooperative or condominium must file a declaration and disclosure statement with the New York Attorney General's office.
6. The co-op members develop house rules for the operation of the cooperative. House rules cover such issues as garbage disposal, maintenance, and noise and conflict resolution. They are generally more detailed than items in the proprietary lease and deal with day-to day behavior of the tenants and general operations.
7. Two processes are used by a cooperative to approve a purchaser: (1) acceptance of the purchaser's package by the board of directors and (2) a private interview between the prospective purchasers and the board of directors.
8. To keep subletting from overtaking the building, most cooperatives that allow subletting limit the timeframe of the sublet.
9. A condop is a building that includes condominium and cooperative ownership in the same structure. The creation of a condop allows property owners to collect a sizable portion of rent from a nonshareholder building tenant and does not violate the IRS 80-20 rule.

10. To create a condominium, the owner of the property (the declarant) records a condominium declaration. The declaration includes certain provisions required by statute. The sponsor records the declaration with the county clerk and the offering plan with the New York Attorney General.

11. The shareholder's rights and obligations are in the condominium's bylaws. A board of managers (or directors) oversees the finances and decision-making policy regarding the property.

12. The sponsor is the owner or developer of the condominium. He must appoint the board of directors and the managing agent and place a limitation on sponsor control of the board.

13. A letter of intent is an agreement to purchase a condominium. The letter is a written offer to reserve a specific unit that may be under construction. Certain sections of the letter may be nonbinding, such as the unit's final price.

14. A lender normally requires at least a temporary CO before it will close the loan. If a temporary certificate of occupancy (TCO) expires and is not renewed, a new buyer may find it difficult or impossible to renew homeowner's insurance policies, sell, or refinance the unit.

15. Flipping may be a problem because it can drive up prices. The investor attempts to buy low and sell high. It can cause major losses for people who buy the flipped property from the investor and end up paying more than if they bought it from the developer.

16. The title company completes a title search before purchase. The search reveals any defects in the title of the unit along with any problems or liens against the condominium building or the complex.

17. Condominium contracts are similar to other fee simple interest real estate contracts. However, they may contain a right of first refusal clause for the board of managers of a condominium association.

18. Closing costs for the seller include the NYC Real Property Transfer Tax (if applicable) and NYS Real Property Transfer Tax, broker's commission, managing agent's fees, UCC-3 filing fee, and attorney's fees. The cooperative corporation may charge a flip tax and a stock transfer fee. Closing costs for the buyer include the UCC-1 filing fee, mortgage recording tax (for condos), title search and title policy, managing agent's fees, credit report fees, attorney's fees, and Mansion Tax (if applicable.)

Commercial and Investment Properties

Key Terms

After-tax cash flow The profit from income-producing property, less income taxes, if any, attributable to the property's income

Anchor tenant A well-known commercial retail business, such as a national chain store or regional department store, placed in a shopping center to generate the most customers for all stores in the shopping center

Capitalization rate The annual return that an investor expects to receive; the primary method to estimate the present value of income producing properties

Cash flow The net proceeds after all expenses are met; may be measured *before* or *after* taxes are considered

Cash-on-cash return The ratio of annual before-tax cash flow to the total amount of cash invested, expressed as a percentage.

Common areas Includes the lobby, elevators, corridors, restrooms, and utility closets; tenants may pay a pro rata share for the common areas in addition to their own space

Debt service Mortgage principal and interest payments

Effective gross income Total potential income, less deductions for vacancy and credit losses, plus other income

Feasibility study A detailed economic analysis that considers the cost of site development, construction, financing, tax considerations, rates of return on similar investments, and the benefit to the community

Gross income Income received without subtracting expenses

Lease escalation clauses Increased costs to the tenant for different reasons at specified times during the lease term

Leverage The use of borrowed funds in addition to an investor's own funds

Net operating income Gross operating income minus operating expenses and debt service (cash flow)

Operating statement A report of rental property receipts and disbursements, resulting in net income

Porter's wage escalation formula Provides that the rent will increase a specific amount per square foot for a specified increase in the porter's hourly wage

Pro-forma schedule An operating statement that reflects a property's income and expenses based upon the investor's expectations about the real estate market

Rate of return Percentage of income that the investor gets back on an investment

Rentable square footage Equals the entire space including the usable square footage and the tenant's pro-rata share of the building common areas, such as the lobby, hallways, and restrooms

Tax shelter A method of protecting income from taxation; for example, by accelerating allowable depreciation

Time value of money The principle that the passage of time affects the value of a given sum by earning interest and by being eroded by inflation

Usable square footage The area contained within the space that the tenant occupies

Key Points

1. Types of investment property include unimproved land, residential building, multi-use buildings, retail centers, and offices.

2. The investor wants to generate income (cash flow) without taking a substantial risk.

3. Leverage is the use of borrowed funds. Leverage allows the investor to accumulate the maximum amount of real estate with the minimum amount of personal funds.

4. Before investing, an investor must consider the time value of money, that is, where his investment funds will bring the greatest return on dollars invested for a given period.

5. The rate of return, or percentage of income per dollar amount invested, that the investor gets back on an investment includes a risk factor. The greater the risk of loss, the greater the potential rate of return the investor can expect.

6. The result of deducting operating expenses is net operating income. Mortgage principal and interest payments are called debt service.

7. Cash flows, or income dollars received, are the most important considerations in evaluating an investment. The investor evaluates cash flows before and after taxes.

8. There are two types of income to consider: cash flows during the holding period of the investment and cash generated when the property is sold at the end of the holding period.

9. Cash-on-cash return is a value measurement for a property that considers the equity in the property measured against the cash flow. The method looks at the amount of cash required to purchase the equity interest in a property—the difference between the sales price and the mortgage loan. It also measures the cash flow.

10. A capitalization rate is the annual return that an investor expects to receive. The capitalization rate is used in the appraisal income approach. It is the primary method used to estimate the present value of income-producing properties. The capitalization formula is value × capitalization rate = annual net income.

11. The rentable square footage of most commercial space includes square footage that cannot be used or sometimes seen, but that tenant pays rent for anyway. Rentable square footage includes the usable square footage and the tenant's pro rata share of the building common areas, such as the lobby, hallways, and restrooms.

12. Tenant costs may include common area maintenance (CAM) costs for areas such as the lobby, elevators, corridors, restrooms, and utility closets.

13. A business client is generally committed to a longer lease term and a more expensive lease. Unlike residential leases, there is no standard commercial lease agreement. Each lease conforms to the particular space and tenant.

14. Lease clauses include use clauses; subordination, nondisturbance, and attornment clauses; estoppel certificates; sublease/ assignment clauses, and electric service clauses.

15. Lease escalation clauses call for increased costs to the tenant for different reasons at specified times during the lease term. These clauses protect the property owner against increases in operating costs.

16. Lease escalation clauses include definitions for proportionate share of occupancy and base year, operating stop and tax stop clauses, real property tax clauses, direct operating costs, the Porter's Wage Escalation formula, and fixed percentage increases.

Income Tax Issues in Real Estate Transactions

Key Terms

Active income Salaries or income from a business in which the taxpayer materially participates

Adjusted basis Value of property used to determine the amount of gain or loss realized by an owner upon sale of the property; equals acquisition cost plus capital improvements minus depreciation taken

Appreciation An increase in value

Basis Usually the cost of a property

Boot Cash received in a tax-deferred exchange

Capital gain The profit realized from the sale of real estate or other investment

Capital loss Occurs when an investment property or other type of investment is sold

Cost recovery A type of income tax deduction available for real estate and personal

Deductible expenses Cost of operating a property used in business or held as an investment; these expenses are subtracted from gross income to arrive at net income

Depreciated value The basis of a depreciable asset, used to compute the taxable gain from its sale; the basis is acquisition cost, plus capital improvements, less accrued depreciation

Economic depreciation Loss of value from physical deterioration of property caused by normal use, damage caused by natural and other hazards, and failure to maintain the property adequately

Passive activity A trade or business in which the taxpayer invests but does not materially participate

Passive activity income Income from funds invested in passive activities

Portfolio income Interest, annuities, dividends, royalties, and profits from the sale of portfolio assets

Recaptured depreciation When a property owner disposes of the property, a tax on the income or gain realized because of the allowed depreciation is recaptured as ordinary income up to the amount of the depreciation; recapture means to be included as taxable income.

Straight-line depreciation A type of income tax depreciation that allows investment property to be deducted in installments over a number of years

Tax basis Consists of the price paid for the property, plus expenses incurred in acquiring the property (other than those incurred in arranging financing), plus the costs of any capital improvements

Tax depreciation A deduction from a property's income when determining taxable income

Tax-deferred exchange Trading of like-kind properties held as an investment or for business use.

Key Points

1. There are seven tax brackets for federal income tax: 0, 10, 15, 25, 28, 33, and 35 percent. Most taxpayers fall between the 15 and 28 percent tax brackets.

2. The "Age 59½ Rule" allows first-time homebuyer to use IRA distributions to fund up to $10,000 of their new home cost. They do not have to pay the 10 percent early distribution penalty.

3. Property taxes may be deducted on any type of real property including a personal residence, a second home, a time-share, vacant land, income property, and inherited property.

4. A mortgage must be a secured debt on a qualified home for a taxpayer to take out a home mortgage interest deduction. Interest paid on investment property is generally fully deductible.

5. Capital gain is the profit realized from real estate investment. Capital loss occurs when an investment sells at a loss. The long-term capital gain tax is 15 percent when the taxpayer's rate is above the 15 percent income bracket. The gain is taxed at 5 percent when the taxpayer is in the 15 percent bracket or below.

6. According to the tax code, single taxpayers may take up to a $250,000 exclusion from taxation on gain in the sale of their homes. Married taxpayers may take up to a $500,000 exclusion.

7. The adjusted basis of a property consists of the price paid for the property. It also includes expenses incurred in acquiring the property and the cost of any capital improvements (less depreciation if applicable).

8. There are three classifications of income: active income earned through salaries or in a business in which the taxpayer actively participates; portfolio income, which includes interest, annuities, dividends, and royalties; and passive activity income, that includes invested funds.

9. A passive activity involves conducting any trade or business in which the taxpayer does not actively participate. This includes rental activities and limited partnerships.

10. When a taxpayer disposes of property, a tax on the income or gain realized because of the allowed depreciation is recaptured as ordinary income up to the amount of the depreciation. Real estate sold after May 7, 1997, is recaptured at a 25 percent rate.

11. To qualify as a tax-deferred exchange, like-kind property must be exchanged. The property exchanged must have been held for use in business (other than inventory) or as an investment.

12. When an exchangor receives cash or some other type of nonqualifying property in addition to like-kind property, the transaction may still partially qualify as a tax-deferred exchange. The cash in the exchange is called the boot.

13. Interest may be deducted for home acquisition and home equity financing, home improvement loans, and construction financing.

14. A buyer can deduct points charged for mortgage financing in the year paid or over the life of the mortgage depending on whether the points charged meet certain IRS tests. Prepayment penalty charges may be tax-deductible. Other closing expenses are not generally tax-deductible.

15. Tax depreciation is a deductible allowance from net income used to arrive at taxable income. It provides a tax shelter for the property owner.

16. Depreciation enables the owner of a business or an investment property to recover the cost or other basis of the asset. Land is not depreciable—only structures on the land.

Mortgage Brokerage

Key Terms

Mortgage bankers Individuals and entities licensed by the New York Banking Department to make residential mortgage loans; applies to one- to four-unit properties

Mortgage brokers Individuals and entities registered by the New York Banking Department to solicit, process, place, or negotiate residential mortgage loans for others; applies to one- to four-unit properties

Mortgage Broker Dual Agency Disclosure Form A banking department form required when a person is acting as a mortgage broker and a real estate broker in the same transaction

Mortgage commitment A promise made by a lending institution to make a certain type of mortgage loan

Nonconforming loan A loan that does not meet Federal Reserve Bank criteria for funding. The reason may be that the loan amount is a higher dollar amount than the conforming loan limit

Preapplication and Fee Agreement According to the Banking Law, a mortgage broker or mortgage banker must provide certain disclosures to each applicant for a mortgage loan, at or before the time of application. These disclosures include the fees payable at the time of application, the conditions for refunding the fee, and if the mortgage broker is using three or fewer lenders; this form complies with the Banking Law

Preapproval A step above pre-qualification; involves verifying a purchaser's credit, down payment, and employment history

Prequalification Not a commitment by the lender; after the loan officer determines that a purchaser pre-qualifies, he issues a pre-qualification letter that is used to make an offer on a property and show the seller that the purchaser qualifies to buy the property.
Rate lock A mortgage loan cannot be closed without locking in an interest rate

Service release premium A form of compensation that a lender may pay to a broker for delivering a loan; each loan comes with a servicing right to collect the mortgage payments

Underwriting The process in which the lender evaluates all of the borrower's financial data and determines if the borrower will obtain the loan

Yield spread premium (also known as a **lender rebate**) is the rate at which a mortgage broker is compensated for the difference between the interest rate on a par loan and the interest rate on an above par loan that a mortgage broker can deliver to the lender; this is expressed in the number of points paid to a mortgage broker

Key Points

1. In New York, a mortgage broker must register with the New York State Banking Department.

2. A licensed real estate broker may use his broker license to become a registered mortgage broker. The real estate broker license must be current. Licensed salespersons must have actively participated in the residential mortgage business for two years.

3. According to New York banking regulations, when a mortgage broker representing the buyer/borrower also is the real estate broker representing the seller in the same residential real estate transaction, that information must be disclosed at the first substantive contact between the mortgage broker and the purchaser/borrower. A prescribed Banking Department Dual Agency Disclosure Form is used.

4. A mortgage broker acting as a real estate broker in the same transaction must use the disclosure form for real estate transactions and the disclosure form for mortgage broker transactions for covered properties.

5. A mortgage banker is an individual or a company licensed by the New York Banking Department to engage in the business of making residential mortgage loans. Mortgage bankers, also called mortgage companies, make mortgage loans for housing construction and the purchase of existing housing.

6. The requirements for a mortgage banker license include having a net worth of at least $250,000 and having an existing line of credit of at least $1 million provided by a banking institution, an insurance company, or a similar credit facility approved by the Superintendent of Banking.

7. The role of the mortgage broker is to find appropriate financing at the most favorable interest rate and terms for a borrower.

8. A mortgage broker may arrange for a prequalification or preapproval letter. He suggests the best financing options, coordinates the appraisal, and helps obtain the mortgage commitment.

9. Mortgage brokers analyze and find a variety of mortgage products that may be applicable to a certain borrower. These products include amortized mortgages, adjustable rate mortgages, construction loans, and conforming and nonconforming loans,

10. Some mortgage brokers process loans and close loans in their own name. However, at or about the time of settlement, they transfer these loans to lenders that simultaneously advance funds for the loans. This transaction is known in the lending industry as table funding.

11. Mortgage brokers assist with other closing details such as making sure the loan is available, the certificate of occupancy is issued, and bank conditions are satisfied.

12. A mortgage broker chooses from a variety of available lenders to secure a deal for the borrower. For example, when a purchaser obtains a mortgage loan, it may be possible to lock in a certain interest rate. This lock-in can be achieved with traditional lenders as well.

13. The mortgage broker's commission is paid by the borrower or more likely by the lender. The fee increases the loan balance and is paid through a lender's rebate (yield spread premium or service release premium). The mortgage broker's fee must be disclosed to the borrower.

Property Management

Key Terms

Actual eviction The removal of a tenant by the landlord because the tenant breached a condition of a lease or other rental contract

Capital expense Capital expenses are those required to improve or maintain a building

Capital reserve budget A projected budget over the economic life of the improvements of the property set aside to cover variable expenses such as repairs, decorating, remodeling, and capital improvements

Constructive eviction Results from some action or inaction by the landlord that renders the premises unsuitable for the use agreed to in a lease or other rental contract

Corrective maintenance Work performed to fix a nonfunctioning item that the tenant has reported; example, repair of a leaky faucet

Eviction A landlord's action that interferes with the tenant's use or possession of the property; eviction may be actual or constructive

Fixed expenses Expenditures such as property taxes, license fees, and property insurance; subtracted from effective gross income to determine net operating income

Insurable interest The legitimate financial interest an insured has in a property that provides eligibility for insurance coverage of any type

Management agreement A contract that creates an agency relationship in which the owner is the principal and the property manager is the agent for the purposes specified in the agreement

Management proposal A document that sets forth the duties of the manager if employed by the owner

Operating budget An annual budget that includes only the items of income and expense expected for week-to-week operation

Planned Unit Development (PUD) A form of cluster zoning providing for both residential and commercial land uses within a zoned area

Preventative maintenance Requires a periodic check of mechanical equipment on the premises to minimize wear and tear; for example, changing air filters on air conditioners and furnaces

Property management report A periodic (usually monthly) accounting of all funds received and disbursed; contains detailed information of all receipts and expenditures for the period covered (plus the year-to-date) and relates each item to the operating budget for the period

Property management The leasing, marketing, managing, maintenance, and accounting functions necessary to operate a commercial property

Property manager A person who manages properties as an agent of the owner

Public liability insurance Covers the risks an owner assumes when the public enters his premises

Resident manager A person living on the premises who is a paid employee of the owner

Risk management Embodies the concern for controlling and limiting risk in property ownership

Stabilized budget A forecast of income and expenses reasonably projected over a short term, typically five years

Variable expense An expense that is not specifically predictable and is subject to the needs of a property at any given time

Key Points

1. The property manager strives to produce the greatest net return possible for the owner.
2. When an individual is employed by one owner of real property on a salaried basis to perform any of the functions of a real estate salesperson or broker defined in the New York Real Property Law, he does not require a real estate license.
3. If an individual or a company works for more than one owner, the individual or company should have a real estate license. If the individual or company has a broker license, the people working for the company would have salesperson licenses.
4. A building manager may work for a property management firm or have his own company.
5. A resident manager lives on the premises and is a salaried employee of the owner. A real estate broker, a management firm, or an owner of a building may employ the resident manager.
6. Real estate asset managers act as the property owner's advisor for the property. They plan and direct the purchase, development, and sale of real estate on behalf of the business and investors. They focus on long-term financial planning rather than on day-to-day operations of the property.
7. The property manager acts as the owner's agent and fiduciary in managing renting, leasing, and perhaps selling the property.
8. When a property manager enters into a management agreement, a general agency is created. The manager owes a fiduciary (undivided loyalty) responsibility to his principal. The manager owes undivided loyalty to the owner-principal.
9. Risk management describes the concern for controlling and limiting risk in property ownership. A manager's written specifications to competing agents ensure comparable quotes.
10. Property managers fulfill their basic responsibilities by formulating a management plan; handling rentals, tenant relations, and employees; overseeing the budget; paying bills; and supervising maintenance.
11. The property manager must be skilled in a number of areas, including accounting, budgeting, construction and building systems, and owner-tenant relations. Real estate-related knowledge is essential.
12. Properties that may require management are condominiums, cooperatives, apartments, single-family rental houses, mobile home parks, office buildings, shopping malls, industrial property, and farms.
13. The overall goals of the property manager are to (a) produce the best possible net operating income from the property and (b) increase the value of the principal's investment.
14. The property manager must continuously evaluate rents, budgets, and markets to ensure the best future return on the investment.
15. An operating budget, capital reserve budget, and stabilized budget should be established before rental f a project is organized and structured. The budgets are subject to adjustments, particularly in the first months of a project.

16. The operating statement is a method that property owners use to project net operating income for a property. Net operating income (NOI) is the gross income minus the operating expenses.

17. Public relations serve two roles in the property management office. A management company uses public relations to market itself, and property managers use public relations to market client properties.

18. The property management report is a periodic accounting that a property manager provides to the property owner.

Quick View Tables

The following *quick view* tables contain important study information from each of the subjects in the salespersons 75-hour course.

License Law and Regulations

Table 1. A Summary of License Requirements

Requirement	Salesperson	Broker/ Associate Broker
Age	18	20
Citizenship/permanent residency	Yes, other choices	Yes
Qualifying course	75 hours	120 hours total
Experience	None	2 years as salesperson or 3 years' equivalent
Fee/term of license	$50/2 years	$150/2 years
Continuing Ed	22.5/every 2 years	22.5/every 2 years
Licensing agency	Dept of State	Dept of State
License Law	Article 12-A of the Real Property Law	Article 12-A of the Real Property Law

Law of Agency

Table 2. A Types of Agents

Type of Agent	Representation	Definition	Limitations
1. Single agent	Buyer or seller	The agent works for the buyer or seller.	The agent never represents both. Firms that represent solely the buyer or seller may reject subagency and dual agency. The broker should counsel, but not advise the principal as to the limitations of this relationship. If a situation arises to compromise the relationship, the broker could suggest that another broker from a referral firm be utilized.
2. Seller agent	Seller	A listing agent who acts alone or cooperates with other agents as a subagent or broker's agent.	The agent works in the best interests of the seller but must deal fairly and honestly with buyers.
3. Subagent	Seller or buyer	An agent of the principal under the agency relationship of the primary broker.	The agent must be hired with the principal's informed consent. The principal may be vicariously liable for the acts of the subagent.
4. Buyer agent	Buyer	The agent represents the buyer as principal and enters into a listing agreement with the buyer. Locates a property and negotiates for the buyer.	The agent works in the best interests of the buyer but must deal fairly and honestly with sellers.
5. Dual agent	Buyer and seller	Represents both buyer and seller in the same transaction; undisclosed dual agency is a breach of fiduciary duty and violation of license law.	This arrangement is allowable only with disclosure and written informed consent. The agent cannot give undivided loyalty to either party.
6. Brokers agent	Broker (who may represent either buyer or seller)	A broker's agent cooperates with or is engaged by a listing agent, buyer's agent, or tenant's agent. The seller, buyer, landlord, or tenant does not have vicarious liability for the acts of the broker's agent.	The broker's agent does not have a direct relationship with the seller, buyer, landlord, or tenant.

Table 2.A Continued.	Type of Agent	Representation	Definition	Limitations
	7. Cooperating Agent	Buyers or sellers	Representation includes seller agents, subagents, buyer agents, and broker's agents. These agents work to assist the listing broker in the sale of the property. Cooperating agents may or may not work through MLS.	The principal can designate those agents that work as broker's agents, subagents, or buyer agents. The principal may choose to reject subagency arrangements.

Independent Contractor

Table 2.B Requirements for Salesperson Independent Contractor Status

Requirement	Parties involved
NYS salesperson or broker license	Regulated by NYS Department of State
Independent contractor agreement	Between salesperson and broker
Termination of relationship	Agreement between salesperson and broker at any time

Estates and Interests

Table 3. A Types of ownership

Type	Owners	Right of Survivorship
In severalty	One owner	No
Tenancy in common	Two or more	No
Joint tenancy	Two or more	Yes

Liens and Easements

Table 3.B 1 . Types of Liens

Type	Specific/General	Voluntary/Involuntary
Mortgage	Specific	Voluntary
Real property tax	Specific	Involuntary
Mechanic's	Specific	Involuntary
Judgment	General	Involuntary
Income tax	General	Involuntary

Table 3.B 2 . Types of Easements

Type of easement	Purpose	Owner
Easement in gross	Utilities	Government/public company
Easement appurtenant	Ingress/egress	Private parties
Negative easement appurtenant	View easements	Private parties

Deeds

Table 3.C Forms of Deeds

Type	Description
Full covenant and warranty	Fullest guarantee of title
Quitclaim	No warranties of title
Bargain and sale with covenants	Contains warranties of title
Judicial deed	Results from a court order

Title Closing and Costs

Table 3. D

Closing Preparations

Required for Closing	Definition
Closing statement	Prepared by attorneys for buyer, seller, and lender
Licensee assistance	Inspection of property with purchaser before closing
Marketable title	Includes title search, check for chain of title, abstract of title
Payment of broker commission	Paid at closing; may include all or part of deposit
Perc, soil, water flow tests	New construction and other property that have wastewater treatment or well
Place of closing	Lender, attorney office, title company, county clerk
Structural inspection	Performed by NYS licensed home inspector, other professionals
Title Insurance	Insures the policy owner against financial loss if title is not good

Leases

Table 4.A Lease Agreements

Term	Definition
Assignment	Full transfer of lease by lessee to another who pays owner
Sublease	Sublessee pays leaseholder who pays owner
Actual eviction	Illegal forcible eviction of tenant
Constructive eviction	Tenant may withhold rent if necessary services not provided (requires court order)
Eviction	Legal proceeding to evict a tenant

Contracts

Table 4.B Types of contracts

Express	Oral or written agreement
Implied	Inferred from behavior of the parties
Unilateral	One party is obligated under the contract
Bilateral	Two parties are obligated under the contract
Executory	Not fully performed contract
Executed	Fully performed contract
Valid	Binding and enforceable
Void	No legal force or effect
Voidable	May or may not be enforceable

Contract Preparation

Table 4.C Data Required for Contract Preparation

Data	Supplied By
Certificate of Occupancy	Building Department
Personal Data	Buyer , Seller, Real Estate Agent
Prior Deed	Seller
Prior Title Insurance Policy	Seller, Lender
Survey	Seller or Buyer (new survey may be required)
Tax , water, fuel bills	Seller through his agent

Real Estate Finances (Mortgages)

Table 5 Mortgage Summary

Mortgage type	Definition	Participants
Primary mortgage market	Mortgages obtained from lender	Any bank or other lending institution
Secondary mortgage market	Mortgages purchased from lender by secondary market agencies	Fannie Mae, Ginnie Mae, Freddie Mac
Conventional loans	Loans not insured by a government agency	Any bank or other lending institution
Government loans	Loans insured by a government agency	Lenders that process FHA, VA, RHS, SONYMA loans
Conforming loans	Loan applications that conform to secondary market guidelines	Fannie Mae, Ginnie Mae, Freddie Mac
Seller financing	Seller takes a mortgage for all or part of the purchase price	Sellers that participate in purchase money, wrap-around mortgages, installment land contracts, or sale leaseback

Land Use Regulations

Table 6 Public Control of Land

Control	Definition	Method
Eminent domain	Government right to take property for public good	Condemnation-act of taking
Taxation	Levy against property value	Lien against property
Police Power	Right of government to act for public welfare	All public laws, regulations, and agencies
Escheat	Right of government to seize property if there are no heirs	Government follows protocol to locate heirs

Construction

Table 7.A Main Building Systems Defined

System	Purpose
Electrical system	Begins outside with service entrance cables that connect to the main panel board. Branch circuit wires bring electrical power to receptacles.
Heating system	Consist of either hot water, steam, forced warm air, or electric furnaces. Fueled by oil, gas, solar, or electricity.
HVAC system	Heating, ventilating, and cooling system
Insulation System	Insulation is applied to the warm (inside) of exterior walls such as roofs, ceilings, floors, and foundation walls.
Plumbing system	Actually two piping systems; one delivers clean water into the structure; the other processes wastewater
Private wastewater system	Also called a septic system, it processes and treats wastewater on site.
Private water supply system	Consists of well or wells pumping water from the ground to a pressurized holding tank.

Environmental Issues

Table 7.B The Residential Leadbased Paint Hazard Reduction Act

Main Point	Explanation
Property types	Sale or lease of residential properties built before 1978
Who must comply	Sellers and seller agents
Forms needed	Lead hazard pamphlet, reports of leadbased paint, contingency for 10-day lead paint assessment, disclosure form
Penalty for non compliance	Payment of up to 3 times the amount of damage incurred by lessor or purchaser; up to $10,000 fine

Valuation Process and Pricing Properties

Table 8 Comparing Market Value, Price, and Cost

Type of Value	Definition
Market value	The price a property will bring in a competitive market with neither party under duress
Price	The amount of money a purchaser and seller agrees upon
Cost	The dollar expenditure for labor, materials, other items

Human Rights and Fair Housing

Table 9 Human Rights Law Violations

Violation	Definition	Possible Violator
Blockbusting	Behavior that causes panic selling by announcing that people of certain protected classes are moving to the neighborhood; an attempt to gain listings	Salespersons, Brokers
Steering	Behavior that encourages prospects either toward or away from certain communities based on membership in certain protected classes	Salespersons, Brokers
Redlining	Certain neighborhoods are targeted as ones that are not eligible for mortgages or other home loans based on the community's membership in certain protected classes	Lenders

Real Estate Mathematics

Table 10 Table of Important Measures and Formulas

Measure	Formula
Acre	43,560 sq. ft.
Area of rectangle	Width x depth
Area of a triangle	$1/2$ base x height
Interest	Loan balance x interest rate = annual interest
Commission	Sales price paid x percentage of commission = commission

Municipal Agencies

Table 11 List of Municipal Agencies

Agency	Level of Government
Architectural Review Board	City, Town, Village
Building Department	City, Town, Village
City/Town Council	City/Town
Conservational Advisory Council/ Wetlands Commission	County, City, Town, Village
Engineer	City, Town, Village
Health Department	City, County
Planning Board	Town, City, Village, County
Tax Assessor	City, Town, Village
Village Board of Trustees	Village
Zoning Board of Appeals	City, Town, Village

Property Insurance

Table 12 Types of Insurance

Type of Insurance Policy	Purpose
Commercial	Liability and property insurance and possible business suspension insurance
Contents	Issued on an actual cash basis, must pay extra for replacement cost
Flood	Issued to property owners in coastal and other flood prone areas
Homeowners	Varying levels of coverage insuring the home and contents
Tenants	Generally applies to improvements within the unit, not the building
Umbrella	Excess liability policy for additional coverage above primary policy

Taxes and Assessments

Table 13 When Reassessment May Occur

Reassessment	Explanation
Community wide reassessment	Periodically to restore fairness within the community
Illegal/ legal assessment	Taxpayer may protest unequal or unlawful assessment
Obtaining a building permit	Improvement made to property, finished basement, pool, garage
Reassessment upon sale	Property may not be reassessed immediately upon purchase but at a later date for fairness
Undeclared improvements discovered	Assessor cross-checks building permits

Condominiums and Cooperatives

Table 14 Ownership Differences and Similarities between a Condominium and a Cooperative

Cooperatives	Condominiums
Leasehold ownership	Fee simple ownership
Board package and interview	Purchaser documents and interview but may not be as strict as coop
By laws and house rules	Covenants, conditions, and restrictions, and bylaws
Common areas owned by cooperative cooperation	Common area owned in common by owners of individual units
Monthly maintenance fee to cooperative for underlying mortgage, other expenses	Common charges for upkeep, insurance, and salaries
Offering plan must be approved by attorney general	Offering plan must be approved by attorney general
Possible flip tax at closing	No flip tax
Proprietary lease and shares of stock in cooperative corporation	Deed

Commercial and Investment Real Estate

Table 15 Commercial Lease Clauses

Lease Clause	Purpose
Building amenities	Moving allowances, parking, other incentives
Escalation clauses	Various types of clauses indicating terms of lease payment increases
Estoppel certificate	Tenant's statement pertaining to the lease term , rent, security, and other issues
Lease Duration	Short-term leases generally 3-5 years; long term, 5 or more years
On-site management	Degree of maintenance coverage
Subordination, nondisturbance, and attornment agreement	Legal agreements pertaining to the lease
Tenant mix	Variety of businesses in the building
Type of lease	Triple net, net, gross, percentage
Use clause	Limitations as to how space can be used

Income Tax Issues in Real Estate Transactions

Table 16 Like-Kind (Tax Deferred) Exchange

Issues for a like-kind exchange	Explanation
Any cash (boot) received in the transaction	Transaction may still partially qualify as a tax deferred exchange
Closing of new property	Must close within 180 days from the date exchangor sold the original property
Must be business or investment property	Personal residences, stocks, cars, not allowed
Purchase of replacement property	Investor must contract for replacement property within 45 days
Qualified Intermediary (QI)	The QI accepts funds and handles contracts

Mortgage Brokerage

Table 17 The Differences and Similarities between a Mortgage Broker and a Mortgage Banker

Mortgage Broker	Mortgage Banker
Cannot act as a mortgage banker	Can act as a mortgage broker
Does not collect payments	May collect payments
Finds financing	Provides financing
Receives a fee for finding financing (through borrower, mortgage banker)	Receives payment (points, interest) for providing financing (from borrower)
Registered by NYS Banking Dept	Registered by NYS Banking Dept

Property Management

Table 18 Property Manager's Obligations to the Owner

Obligations	Explanation
Budget	Operating budget, capital reserve budget, variable expenses, stabilized budget
Future of the project	Analyze business trends
Maintenance	Preventative maintenance, corrective maintenance, construction
Rents space, collects rent, pays expenses	Basic functions
Reporting	A periodic accounting of all funds received and disbursed
Tenant relations	Tenant problems, evictions, subletting

Table 19 Remembering the "ors" and "ees" and what they mean

There are many "ors" and "ees" in real estate law. If the word ends in *or*, think of this party as the *giver*, the *seller*, or the *initiator* of something.

If the word ends in *ee*, think of the party as the *receiver*, the *purchaser*, or the *taker* of something.

Examples:

"or"	"ee"
Grantor—gives deed	Grantee—receives deed
Lessor—gives lease	Lessee—receives lease
Optionor-gives option	Optionee—receives option
Mortgagor—borrower gives mortgage (note)	Mortgagee—or lender receives mortgage (note)
Vendor—sells item	Vendee—receives or purchases item

Marcia's List

The following is a quick abbreviated overview of the most important key terms and concepts from each of the topics in the 75-hour salesperson course. Check off the items you are not sure of and look them up in this Cram or *New York Real Estate for Salespersons, 4th e.*

Subject 1 – License Law and Regulations

Article 12-A
Blind Ad
Commingling
Duties that require a license
Exemptions to licensure
Misdemeanor
Net listing
Requirements for licensure
Salesperson/broker/associate broker

Subject 2 – Law of Agency and Independent Contractor

Part I Law of Agency
Agency Disclosure Form
Broker's agent
Client/principal/customer
Designated agent
Dual agent
Exclusive agency
Exclusive-right-to-sell
Fiduciary
First substantive contact
Group boycott
Market allocation agreement
Open listing
Price fixing
Subagent
Tie-in arrangement
Undivided loyalty
Vicarious liability

Part II Independent Contractor
Independent contractor/independent contractor agreement
Internal Revenue Code Section 3508 (a)(b)

Subject 3 – Legal Issues

Part I Estates and Interests
Fee simple absolute
Fixture/trade fixture

Joint tenancy
Leasehold estate
Life estate
Severalty
Tenancy in common

Part II – Liens and Easements
Easement appurtenant
Easement in gross
Encroachment
Encumbrance
Judgment
Lien
Lis pendens
Mechanic's lien

Part III – Deeds
Accession rights
Deed/Conveyance
Delivery and acceptance
Full covenant and warranty deed
Grantor/grantee
Metes and bounds description
Quitclaim deed

Part IV-Title Closing and Costs
Abstract of title/chain of title/title search
Debits/credits
Flip tax
Proration
Real Estate Settlement Procedures Act
Survey

Subject 4 – The Contract of Sale and Leases

Part I Leases
Assignment
Eviction
Gross/net lease
Lessor/lessee
Quiet enjoyment
Sublease

Part II Contracts
Binder
Caveat emptor
Contingencies
Counteroffer
Executory/executed contract
Offer and acceptance
Statute of Frauds

Time is of the essence
Void/voidable, valid contract

Part III Contract Preparation
Attorney review clause
Binder
Down payment
Lawyer's Fund for Client Protection
Mortgage contingency clause

Subject 5 – Real Estate Finance

Amortization
Balloon mortgage
Buydown
Discount points
Fannie Mae/Ginnie Mae/Freddie Mac/Secondary mortgage market
FHA and VA insured loans
Foreclosure
Loan-to-value ratio
Mortgagor/mortgagee
Note or bond
Predatory lending
Regulation Z of the Truth in Lending Act
Satisfaction of mortgage
Subprime loan

Subject 6 – Land Use Regulations

Condemnation
Eminent domain
Escheat
Police power
Spot zoning
Transfer of development rights
Variance

Subject 7–Construction and Environmental Issues

Part I Construction
Carbon monoxide/smoke detector affidavit
Eave/fascia/frieze board/soffit
Flashing
Footing
Foundation
Headers
Joists
Pitch
Platform framing
Ridge beam

Slab-on-grade construction
Voltage/amperage

Part II Environmental Issues
Asbestos
CERCLA/Superfund
Environmental impact statement
Lead
Radon
Residential Lead-based Paint Hazard Reduction Act
State Environmental Quality Review Act
Urea formaldehyde foam insulation (UFFI)

Subject 8–Valuation Process and Pricing Properties

Appraisal
Comparative market analysis
Direct/indirect costs
Evaluation
Market value
Sales comparison, income, cost approach
Supply and demand

Subject 9 – Human Rights and Fair Housing

Blockbusting
Cease and desist list
Civil Rights Act of 1866
Fair Housing Act of 1968
Jones vs. Meyer Supreme Court decision
Nonsolicitation order
Protected classes
Redlining
Steering

Subject 10 – Real Estate Mathematics

Acre
Appreciation/Depreciation
Area formulas
Interest
Percentage formulas

Subject 11 – Municipal Agencies

Architectural Review Board
Conservation Advisory Council
Historic Preservation/ Landmark Commission
Planning board

Receiver of Taxes
Village Board of Trustees
Zoning Board of Appeals

Subject 12 – Property Insurance

Actual cash value
Deductible
Liability insurance
Package policy
Replacement cost
Umbrella policy

Subject 13 – Taxes and Assessments

Assessment/Assessor
Assessing unit/ approved assessing unit
Assessed value
Board of Assessment Review (BAR)
Grievance
Residential Assessment Ratio (RAR)
Special assessment/special assessment districts
Tax levy
Tax rate

Subject 14 – Condominiums and Cooperatives

Alteration agreement
By-laws
Common elements
Condominium
Cooperative
Covenants, Conditions and Restrictions (CCRs)
Declaration
House Rules
Maintenance
Offering statement
Proprietary lease/shares of stock
Sponsor

Subject 15– Commercial and Investment Properties

Capitalization rate
Cash flow
Cash-on-cash return
Common areas
Debt service
IRV formula

Lease escalation clauses and other lease clauses
Leverage
Net operating income/gross income
Proforma statement
Rate of return
Tax shelter
Usable square footage/rentable square footage/loss factor

Subject 16– Income Tax Issues in Real Estate Transactions

Active income/ Passive activity income/ portfolio income
Age 59 ½ rule
Basis/adjusted basis
Boot
Capital gain/ $250,000/$500,000 rule
Deducting mortgage interest and points paid at closing
Recaptured depreciation
Tax depreciation
Tax-deferred exchange/like-kind property

Subject 17– Mortgage Brokerage

Difference between mortgage banker/mortgage broker
Lender rebate
Mortgage Broker Dual Agency Disclosure Form
Prequalification/preapproval
Rate lock

Subject 18– Property Management

Capital expense/variable expense
Corrective maintenance /preventive maintenance
Management agreement
Management proposal
Operating budget/capital reserve budget/stabilized budget
Property management report
Resident manager

Questions for Your Review

This section provides 10 review questions for each topic in the 75-hour course. There are 250 questions. Tear out the Answer Sheet on the following pages, and use it to record your responses to the Review Questions. You may want to photocopy the blank answer sheet so that you can use it to review the questions a second time.

To complete the review questions, choose the letter that best answers the question and record that answer on the Answer Sheet. Check your responses using the "Answer Key for Review Questions" at the back of this guide. The explanation for the correct answer is in the Answer Key. Carefully review all incorrect answers. For a complete study experience, use the footnoted references in the Answer Key to find and review the material in the textbook *New York Real Estate for Salespersons, 4th e.*

Answer Sheet for Review Questions

1. _____

2. _____

3. _____

4. _____

5. _____

6. _____

7. _____

8. _____

9. _____

10. _____

11. _____

12. _____

13. _____

14. _____

15. _____

16. _____

17. _____

18. _____

19. _____

20. _____

21. _____

22. _____

23. _____

24. _____

25. _____

26. _____

27. _____

28. _____

29. _____

30. _____

31. _____

32. _____

33. _____

34. _____

35. _____

36. _____

37. _____

38. _____

39. _____

40. _____

41. _____

42. _____

43. _____

44. _____

45. _____

46. _____

47. _____

48. _____

49. _____

50. _____

51. _____

52. _____

53. _____

54. _____

55. _____

56. _____

57. _____

58. _____

59. _____

60. _____

61. _____

62. _____

63. _____

64. _____

65. _____

66. _____

67. _____

68. _____

69. _____

70. _____

71. _____

72. _____

73. _____

74. _____

75. _____

76. _____

77. _____

78. _____

79. _____

80. _____

Answer Sheet for Review Questions, cont.

81. _____	101. _____	121. _____	141. _____
82. _____	102. _____	122. _____	142. _____
83. _____	103. _____	123. _____	143. _____
84. _____	104. _____	124. _____	144. _____
85. _____	105. _____	125. _____	145. _____
86. _____	106. _____	126. _____	146. _____
87. _____	107. _____	127. _____	147. _____
88. _____	108. _____	128. _____	148. _____
89. _____	109. _____	129. _____	149. _____
90. _____	110. _____	130. _____	150. _____
91. _____	111. _____	131. _____	151. _____
92. _____	112. _____	132. _____	152. _____
93. _____	113. _____	133. _____	153. _____
94. _____	114. _____	134. _____	154. _____
95. _____	115. _____	135. _____	155. _____
96. _____	116. _____	136. _____	156. _____
97. _____	117. _____	137. _____	157. _____
98. _____	118. _____	138. _____	158. _____
99. _____	119. _____	139. _____	159. _____
100. _____	120. _____	140. _____	160. _____

Answer Sheet for Review Questions, cont.

161. _____ 181. _____ 201. _____ 221. _____

162. _____ 182. _____ 202. _____ 222. _____

163. _____ 183. _____ 203. _____ 223. _____

164. _____ 184. _____ 204. _____ 224. _____

165. _____ 185. _____ 205. _____ 225. _____

166. _____ 186. _____ 206. _____ 226. _____

167. _____ 187. _____ 207. _____ 227. _____

168. _____ 188. _____ 208. _____ 228. _____

169. _____ 189. _____ 209. _____ 229. _____

170. _____ 190. _____ 210. _____ 230. _____

171. _____ 191. _____ 211. _____ 231. _____

172. _____ 192. _____ 212. _____ 232. _____

173. _____ 193. _____ 213. _____ 233. _____

174. _____ 194. _____ 214. _____ 234. _____

175. _____ 195. _____ 215. _____ 235. _____

176. _____ 196. _____ 216. _____ 236. _____

177. _____ 197. _____ 217. _____ 237. _____

178. _____ 198. _____ 218. _____ 238. _____

179. _____ 199. _____ 219. _____ 239. _____

180. _____ 200. _____ 220. _____ 240. _____

Answer Sheet for Review Questions, cont.

241. _____

242. _____

243. _____

244. _____

245. _____

246. _____

247. _____

248. _____

249. _____

250. _____

Review Questions

License Law and Regulations

1. Which of the following would NOT result in license suspension or revocation?
   a. engaging in fraudulent practices
   b. accepting compensation from more than one party in a transaction without making a full disclosure to all parties
   c. licensees who are not attorneys giving legal advice
   d. licensees accepting a commission from their sponsoring broker

2. Which of the following require a real estate license to engage in real estate practices?
   a. building superintendent for one owner
   b. public officers representing government interests
   c. attorneys licensed in New York
   d. auctioneers selling real property

3. A licensee who deposits an earnest money deposit in his personal checking account instead of in the broker's trust account is guilty of:
   a. conversion
   b. commingling
   c. escheat
   d. prescription

4. A major purpose of the real estate license law is to:
   a. protect the profitability of the real estate brokerage profession
   b. establish minimum standards for multiple listing services
   c. protect the public
   d. protect licensees from dishonest real estate investors

5. How many hours of qualifying education must a broker complete?
   a. 75
   b. 90
   c. 120
   d. 150

6. The regulatory agency that oversees the licensure process in New York is the:
   a. Department of Law
   b. Department of State
   c. Department of Housing and Urban Development
   d. Attorney General's Office

7. The minimum age for salesperson licensure is:
   a. 16
   b. 18
   c. 19
   d. 21

8. Which of the following is NOT a mandatory requirement for salesperson licensure in New York?
   a. successful completion of the 75-hour qualifying course
   b. broker sponsorship
   c. U.S. citizenship
   d. passing the state license examination

9. When transacting real estate business, which of the following documents must be carried by the licensee?
   a. a listing form
   b. driver's license
   c. pocket card
   d. business card

10. Licensees must complete continuing education requirements:
    a. every two years upon license renewal unless exempt
    b. every four years upon license renewal
    c. only if they are salespersons
    d. only if they have been in business for less than 10 years

Law of Agency
Part I Agency

11. A broker's commission is determined by:
    a. reference to maximum guidelines established by the Division of Licensing Services
    b. agreement between the broker and principal
    c. reference to the multiple listing service fee schedule
    d. reference to the Department of State's fee schedule

12. In the sale of one- to four-unit residential real estate, a listing agent must first disclose her status to a prospective buyer:
    a. when a buyer calls the office
    b. only when instructed to by her broker
    c. when the parties enter into a contract of sale
    d. at the first substantive meeting

13. A person empowered to act on behalf of another is called a(n):
    a. a middleman
    b. agent
    c. principal
    d. party of the first part

14. Danielle listed her home with broker Robert. Danielle, however, sold her home without any assistance from broker Robert. A court ruled that Danielle owed Robert a full commission on the sale of her home. This is because:
    a. Robert had an exclusive agency listing agreement
    b. Robert was a seller broker rather than a buyer broker
    c. Robert had an exclusive right to sell listing agreement
    d. Robert had an open listing agreement

15. A buyer broker CANNOT receive compensation for services through which of the following methods? As:
    a. a subagent of the seller
    b. a flat fee from the buyer
    c. a commission split from a listing broker
    d. a combination of a partial flat fee from the buyer and a commission split from the listing broker

16. The agency relationship:
    a. requires the principal to compensate the agent
    b. must be the result of a written agreement
    c. makes the agent responsible for all acts of the principal
    d. is consensual

17. The most common agency relationship that brokers have with their principals are:
    a. special
    b. general
    c. universal
    d. power of attorney

18. In the sale of one- to four-unit residential property, which of the following situations do NOT require the presentation of a disclosure form and a full explanation of the agent's role to a buyer or seller:
    a. when a buyer makes an appointment to see a property
    b. when entering into a listing agreement with a seller
    c. when a seller agent shows a property to a prospective buyer
    d. when prospects walk through an open house without any specific contact with the agent

19. If Sell-It-Quick Real Estate makes a deal with Country Lane Realty to charge the same commission to all prospective sellers, this is called an illegal:
    a. group boycott
    b. price-fixing agreement
    c. market allocation agreement
    d. tie-in arrangement

20. If Give You A Mortgage Company and Sell It Now Realty arrange that customers who purchase a home from Sell It Now will be required to apply for a mortgage through Give You A Mortgage Company, this is called an illegal:
    a.. group boycott
    b. price fixing agreement
    c. market allocation agreement
    d. tie in arrangement

Law of Agency
Part II Independent Contractor

21. In general, most real estate agents are:
    a. independent contractors
    b. employees
    c. free agents
    d. statutory employees

22. In an independent contractor relationship, which of the following is TRUE?
    a. salespersons only receive their commissions twice yearly
    b. salespersons can work for any number of different brokers at the same time without permission of the other sponsoring broker
    c. salespeople are compensated according to hours worked
    d. an associate broker-independent contractor can be an office manager

23. Which of the following regarding the duties of the independent contractor is FALSE? Independent contractors may:
    a. work any hours they choose
    b. terminate the relationship at any time
    c. work from their homes
    d. not showing a property without the presence of the sponsoring broker

24. In order to comply with federal and state independent contractor law, what must the broker and salesperson do?
    a. enter into a written independent contractor agreement
    b. enter into an oral independent contractor agreement
    c. sign a disclosure statement
    d. the salesperson must show the broker evidence that he does not have other outside employment

25. In order to qualify under the independent contractor relationship, which of the following is necessary? The agent must:
    a. be a broker or associate broker
    b. be licensed
    c. have been licensed for at least one year
    d. work at least 25 hours per week

26. Which IRS form must a broker prepare if an independent contractor earns more than $600 per year?
    a. form 1040
    b. schedule C
    c. form 1099 misc.
    d. from 3508 (a) (b)

27. An independent contractor must file which of the following?
    a. yearly federal tax returns only
    b. yearly state tax returns only
    c. no tax returns as the broker will take care of the filing
    d. yearly federal and state tax returns

28. How many years must a broker keep records as to the sale or mortgage of one-to-four unit dwellings?
    a. one year
    b. two years
    c. three years
    d. four years

29. If a salesperson is classified as an independent contractor, which of the following is TRUE? The broker:
    a. has no duty to supervise the salesperson's activities
    b. has a duty to supervise the salesperson's activities
    c. can only supervise those salespersons who are classified as employees
    d. can only supervise work that is performed in the real estate office

30. If a salesperson is classified as an independent contractor, who pays withholding (social security taxes)?
    a. the broker as it is withheld from the salesperson's commission
    b. the seller who pays the commission
    c. the salesperson' s pension plan
    d. the salesperson must take care of his own withholding and other tax obligations

Legal Issues
Part I Estates and Interests

31. The term, estate pur autre vie, refers to:
    a. the estate of a former tenant
    b. an estate owned by the government
    c. an estate managed by an agent
    d. a life estate measured by the life of someone other than the life tenant

32. Which of the following is NOT a characteristic of real property?
    a. indestructibility
    b. uniqueness
    c. mobility
    d. limited availability

33. Ownership as tenants by the entirety is limited to:
    a. families with children
    b. husband and wife
    c. any two individuals whose names appear on a deed
    d. ownership of commercial properties

34. Public parks and historical monuments are examples of which type of real property?
    a. agricultural
    b. residential
    c. commercial
    d. special purpose

35. A life estate can be defined as:
    a. ownership or possession for someone's lifetime
    b. a measure of profit of the estate
    c. the absorption of one estate into another
    d. a leasehold estate

36. Which of the following is NOT a freehold estate?
    a. fee simple absolute
    b. leasehold
    c. fee simple defeasible
    d. fee simple on condition

37. A grantor conveys 100 acres to his daughter, but if the daughter uses the property for commercial purposes, her ownership terminates. This is an example of a(n):
    a. fee simple on condition
    b. estate pur autre vie
    c. leasehold estate
    d. fee simple absolute

38. Ownership in severalty refers to:
    a. ownership by one owner
    b. co-ownership
    c. a financing charge
    d. purchase of optioned property

39. Chattel refers to:
    a. property pledged as security for payment of a debt
    b. personal property
    c. field for cattle to graze
    d. a wife's interest in her husband's real property

40. An interest in land allowing for possession for a definite and limited time is called:
    a. an estate for years
    b. long-term estate
    c. joint tenancy
    d. usury

Legal Issues
Part II Liens and Easements

41. A lien is:
    a. a privilege to do a particular act
    b. the right to enter a parcel of land
    c. a claim that one person has against the property of another for a debt
    d. money paid for compensation to use one's land

42. An easement is a(n):
    a. parcel of land
    b. nonpossessory use of land by another
    c. easier route through a property
    d. structure that facilitates drainage

43. The meaning of the term, lis pendens, is:
    a. that a lawsuit is pending
    b. Latin for "lease period"
    c. a lien against a property
    d. the extent of authority of a court

44. Mortgages are:
    a. involuntary general liens
    b. voluntary general liens
    c. voluntary specific liens
    d. involuntary specific liens

45. A mechanic's lien is a(n):
    a. involuntary general lien
    b. voluntary general lien
    c. voluntary specific lien
    d. involuntary specific lien

46. Although certain types of liens have priority over other types, what other factor determines the priority of payment of the lien? The:
    a. dollar value of the lien
    b. time and date of filing
    c. credit history of the person who is responsible for payment
    d. type of property to which the lien is attached

47. Utility companies generally must obtain which type of easement to run electrical cables or pipe through a property?
    a. easement in gross
    b. easement appurtenant
    c. easement by prescription
    d. easement by grant

48. The land that benefits from an easement appurtenant is called the:
    a. servient tenement
    b. easement in gross
    c. dominant tenement
    d. encumbered property

49. Tree branches that extend over the boundary of one property into another's are called:
    a. easements
    b. created nuisances
    c. acts of nature
    d. encroachments

50. A characteristic of a license to use another's land is that it is:
    a. similar to a lien
    b. the same as an easement
    c. a temporary privilege
    d. a permanent privilege

Legal Issues
Part III Deeds

51. A deed is:
    a. a note payable on demand
    b. an agreement between parties to do certain things
    c. a document in writing, executed and delivered, that conveys title to real property
    d. to bequeath by a will

52. The habendum clause in a deed is the:
    a. forfeiture clause
    b. defeasance clause
    c. "to have and to hold" clause
    d. mortgaging clause

53. A deed that conveys to a grantee an interest in real estate with no warranty of title is called a(n):
    a. full covenant and warranty deed
    b. executor's deed in the form of a full covenant and warranty deed
    c. deed of trust
    d. quitclaim deed

54. When a deed is executed, this means that it is:
    a. delivered
    b. acknowledged
    c. signed by the grantor
    d. corrected

55. The party that conveys title to real property is called the:
    a. grantee
    b. grantor
    c. trustee
    d. party of the second part

56. The legal term for the transfer of property is called:
    a. alienation
    b. subrogation
    c. lis pendens
    d. execution

57. Which of the following is NOT a judicial deed?
    a. sheriff's deed
    b. correction deed
    c. executor's deed
    d. referee's deed

58. A deed description that starts with a point or place of beginning is called a:
    a. description by monument
    b. description by reference
    c. metes and bounds description
    d. description by lot and block

59. When a landowner donates a parcel of land for public use, this is called:
    a. dedication
    b. adverse possession
    c. the right of accession
    d. forced grant

60. A person appointed in a will to carry out its provisions is called the:
    a. testator
    b. legatee
    c. devisor
    d. executor

Legal Issues
Part IV Title Closing and Costs

61. Title to real estate is transferred:
    a. when a contract for purchase and sale is executed by buyer and seller
    b. when financing for the purchaser is approved by the lending institution
    c. upon execution and delivery of a valid deed
    d. after all existing liens are satisfied

62. Generally, in the closing process, attorneys for a lender represent the best interests of the:
    a. lending institution
    b. purchaser
    c. seller
    d. real estate licensee

63. A federal statute that regulates disclosure and closing requirements relative to mortgage loans on residential property is the:
    a. Truth in Lending Act
    b. Interstate Land Sales Act
    c. Fair Credit Disclosure Act
    d. Real Estate Settlement Procedures Act

64. An unbroken transfer of successive titles to real property is called:
    a. movable title
    b. conveyable title
    c. chain of title
    d. attorney's opinion of title

65. The document which shows the measurements, boundaries, and area of property is called a(n):
    a. feasibility study
    b. survey
    c. architectural rendering
    d. plat

66. A condensed history pertaining to the title of a property is called a(n):
    a. abstract of title
    b. chain of title
    c. title insurance
    d. intestate succession search

67. One of the most important roles of a licensee just before closing is to:
    a. examine the deed to make sure it is valid
    b. prepare the closing statement
    c. examine the abstract of title
    d. arrange and accompany a prospective purchaser through a final inspection of the property

68. A New York tax on the conveyance of title to real property is called the:
    a. mortgage recording tax
    b. real estate transfer tax
    c. capital gains tax
    d. sales tax

69. Which of the following are NOT possible buyer debits at closing?
    a. unpaid utility bills
    b. the purchase price
    c. discount points
    d. homeowner's insurance

70. Which of the following are NOT possible seller debits at closing?
    a. delinquent property taxes
    b. existing mortgage
    c. mortgage insurance
    d. purchase money mortgage taken back from buyer

The Contract of Sale and Leases
Part I Leases

71. Which of the following is a key feature of a periodic lease?
    a. it automatically renews for another period unless notice is given to terminate
    b. it is never for more than one year's duration
    c. it is only used for commercial leases
    d. at the death of the landlord or tenant, the heirs of the deceased are not bound by the terms of the lease

72. Which of the following defines the nature of a leasehold estate? It:
    a. provides title to real property
    b. provides possession, but not title to real property
    c. is conveyed by deed
    d. never exists for a fixed period

73. When the duration of the lease is completely unknown when the lease is signed, this is called a(n):
    a. fixed estate
    b. periodic estate
    c. estate at will
    d. freehold estate

74. A tenant who was originally in lawful possession of a premises but refuses to leave after his right to possession terminates is legally called a:
    a. tenant at will
    b. holdover tenant
    c. squatter
    d. trespasser

75. A lease is most generally a type of:
    a. deed
    b. promissory note
    c. contract
    d. option agreement

76. Which of the following is NOT a standard lease provision?
    a. identification of the premises
    b. competency of the parties to contract
    c. specification of rent and payment
    d. specification of a minimum one-year term

77. When Heath looked over the lease to his apartment, it had so many legal terms and unclear language that he had to take it to his attorney for interpretation. This lease:
    a. is perfectly acceptable
    b. should always be read by an attorney before signing
    c. should appear in at least two languages
    d. should be written in a clear and coherent manner using everyday terminology

78. Which of the following is a right of a landlord and does not have to be specified in the lease?
    a. automatic right to inspect the leased premises for any reason
    b. right to remove a tenant from a premises at any time during the lease
    c. right to enter the premises in an emergency such as a fire
    d. right to send repair persons to the premises without permission from the tenant

79. If a tenant must leave a leased premises because of lack of heat, he may be able to forfeit his lease obligations and claim:
    a. constructive eviction
    b. actual eviction
    c. forfeiture
    d. lis pendens

80. If a landlord sells a building containing rental properties, the new owner may:
    a. evict any of the current tenants without cause
    b. raise the rents on the leased premises before termination of the lease
    c. inspect all of the leased premises without permission from the lessees
    d. none of the above

The Contract of Sale and Leases
Part II Contracts

81. Consideration is:
    a. a promise of quiet enjoyment
    b. the giving of something, which need not be monetary value, as an inducement to contract
    c. always expressed as a dollar value
    d. a power of attorney

82. Which of the following is NOT an essential requirement for a real estate contract?
    a. competent parties
    b. consideration
    c. financing contingency
    d. offer and acceptance

83. The rule that requires real estate contracts to be in writing is called:
    a. Statute of Limitations
    b. Real Estate Settlement Procedures Act
    c. Statute of Frauds
    d. Uniform Commercial Code

84. A contract between two parties who have definitely agreed to the contract terms is called a(n):
    a. express unilateral contract
    b. express bilateral contract
    c. implied bilateral contract
    d. implied unilateral contract

85. Under an installment land contract, which of the following does NOT apply?
    a. the purchaser has immediate legal title to the property
    b. it is an express bilateral executory contract
    c. the purchaser is given possession of the property
    d. the purchaser must maintain the property

86. The substitution of a new contract for a prior contract is called:
    a. sublet
    b. assignment
    c. rescission
    d. release

87. In general, a valid written listing agreement between a seller and a real estate agent where a buyer is not found is a(n):
    a. implied contract
    b. void contract
    c. unenforceable contract
    d. executory contract

88. If a sales contract states that "time is of the essence," this means that the contract must be performed:
    a. within a reasonable time period
    b. within one year
    c. on or before the date stipulated on the contract
    d. within three months

89. Which of the following is FALSE regarding an earnest money deposit. It:
    a. shows the sincerity of buyer
    b. legally must accompany an offer to purchase
    c. demonstrates financial capability to raise the money called for in the purchase offer
    d. may serve as possible liquidated damages to the seller if the buyer defaults

90. A contract with a minor is:
    a. automatically void
    b. illegal
    c. unenforceable
    d. voidable by the minor

The Contract of Sale and Leases
Part III Contract Preparation

91. A form of seller financing is a (n):
    a. assumable mortgage
    b. home equity loan
    c. FHA loan
    d. purchase money mortgage

92. A portion of the property's purchase price that is paid in cash and NOT part of the mortgage is the:
    a. binder
    b. down payment
    c. assumable mortgage
    d. mortgage commitment

93. Which of the following is generally the first to sign the contract of sale?
    a. purchaser
    b. seller
    c. seller's attorney
    d. real estate broker or salesperson

94. Rafael, a real estate salesperson, advises his buyer clients not to sign a contract of sale prepared by their attorney because he believes that the "as is" clause in the contract will cause them trouble later. Which of the following is TRUE? Raphael:
    a. can advise his clients as to legal matters as long as they don't have an attorney
    b. can advise his clients about any matters as long as they have signed the agency disclosure form
    c. can advise his clients on all contract matters
    d. is engaging in the illegal practice of law

95. An IOLA account is one held by which of the following?
    a. real estate brokers
    b. attorneys
    c. apartment sharing agents
    d. mortgage brokers

96. The Lawyer's Fund for Client Protection has to do with attorney:
    a. escrow accounts
    b. licensure
    c. relationships with real estate brokers
    d. court appearances

97. In certain upstate areas, should a real estate salesperson take a deposit, which of the following is TRUE? He:
    a. must keep it in his checking account
    b. must lock it in a safe place until the closing
    c. must turn it over to his broker
    d. can keep it as his commission

98. Keri is buying a residential single-family property for $450,000. Generally, what would be the customary deposit?
    a. $15,000
    b. $30,000
    c. $45,000
    d. $75,000

99. At what point is a real estate contract of sale binding?
    a. when it is signed by buyer and seller
    b. when it is signed by buyer and seller and agents for each
    c. when it is reviewed and approved by the attorneys for buyer and seller
    d. at closing

100. Which of the following documents are NOT required for closing?
    a. survey
    b. certificate of occupancy
    c. prior deed
    d. census statement

Real Estate Finance

101. The mortgagor is the:
    a. lender
    b. broker
    c. borrower
    d. trustee

102. The mortgagee is the:
    a. lender
    b. broker
    c. borrower
    d. trustee

103. A mortgage is a(n):
    a. unilateral implied contract for repayment of a loan
    b. written document pledging a property as security for the repayment of a loan
    c. insurance policy to protect against a variety of hazards
    d. conveyance used to transfer title to real property

104. Which of the following best describes down payments for VA loans? They:
    a. are always 5% of the appraised value
    b. are typically $5,000
    c. are always 10% of the sales price
    d. do not always require a minimum down payment

105. A balloon mortgage is best described as:
    a. based on the borrower's ability to pay
    b. having a larger payment due at the end of its term
    c. covering more than one parcel of real property
    d. an amortized loan

106. When a lender is willing to lower the interest rate at the time the loan is made in return for extra payments of points up front, this is called:
    a. buydown
    b. usury
    c. apportionment
    d. satisfaction of mortgage

107. An amortized mortgage loan is one that is paid in monthly payments:
    a. with a balloon payment at the end
    b. of interest only
    c. of principal only
    d. of both principal and interest

108. A wraparound mortgage:
    a. covers both the mortgaged property and mortgage insurance
    b. covers more than one parcel of real estate
    c. is a subordinate mortgage which includes the same principal obligation secured by a first mortgage against the same property
    d. is a type of purchase money mortgage

109. A document for recording and acknowledging that a mortgage is paid in full is called a(n):
    a. payoff statement
    b. satisfaction
    c. HUD Form No. 1
    d. certificate of title

110. The New York agency that raises money from tax free bonds and applies the money to mortgage loans is called:
    a. Fannie Mae
    b. SONYMA
    c. FDIC
    d. RHA

Land Use Regulations

111. Which of the following is generally TRUE?
    a. escheat is the power of government to take private property for public purposes
    b. zoning ordinances are private land use controls
    c. deed restrictions are examples of the government's right to control land use
    d. eminent domain allows government to take property for public use only if it is for the use and benefit of the public

112. The doctrine of laches refers to:
    a. loss of legal rights because of failure to assert them
    b. a special real estate lockbox
    c. government restrictions on land use
    d. a lessor's interest in leased property

113. The New York law that protects residents in the purchase of vacant subdivided land sold on the installment plan is:
    a. Article 12-A of the Real Property Law
    b. Article 9-A of the Real Property Law
    c. the General Business Law
    d. the Statute of Frauds

114. When property reverts to the state due to the lack of heirs, it is called:
    a. eminent domain
    b. equity
    c. escheat
    d. reversion

115. The agency that coordinates information relevant to an environmental impact statement is called the:
    a. office of the county clerk
    b. zoning board of appeals
    c. lead agency
    d. coordinating agency

116. Zoning ordinances are an example of the use of a government's:
    a. police power
    b. health regulatory power
    c. right of eminent domain
    d. private restrictions

117. Which government agency sends inspectors on-site to insure construction code compliance:
    a. zoning board of appeals
    b. U.S. Department of HUD
    c. Department of Environmental Conservation
    d. building department

118. An in-law apartment that is connected to a residential home is called a(n):
    a. annexation
    b. accessory use
    c. home occupation
    d. group home

119. Hospitals, schools, and courthouses are examples of which type of zoning?
    a. institutional
    b. industrial
    c. public open space
    d. commercial

120. A municipality that imposes a delay in developing property in a given area has issued a(n):
    a. transfer of development rights
    b. moratorium
    c. demographic evaluation
    d. infrastructure assessment

Construction and Environmental Issues

Part I Construction

121. Guidelines for minimum separation distances between a well and a septic system are furnished by the:
    a. Environmental Protection Agency
    b. NYS Department of Environmental Conservation
    c. U.S. Department of HUD
    d. NYS Department of Health

122. Which of the following is NOT a consideration in the design and development of a construction site?
    a. drainage
    b. appurtenances
    c. insulation requirements
    d. zoning

123. The concrete base below the frost line that supports the foundation of a structure is called the:
    a. foundation wall
    b. footing
    c. slab
    d. girder

124. The wooden skeleton of a residential property is called the:
    a. frame
    b. walls
    c. sheetrock
    d. foundation

125. Openings for doors and windows in a residential property are supported by:
    a. lally columns
    b. rafters
    c. headers
    d. the sill plate

126. Which of the following is TRUE?
    a. the lesser the degree of insulation, the greater the R-factor
    b. the greater the degree of insulation, the greater the R-factor
    c. R-factor ratings apply only to blanket insulation
    d. the R-factor has nothing to do with insulation

127. A type of heating system that heats water in a boiler and then uses circulator pumps to propel the heated water to convectors is called a(n):
    a. forced warm air system
    b. electric heating system
    c. heat pump
    d. hot water system

128. Which of the following is FALSE regarding the plumbing system?
    a. the systems for water supply and wastewater are combined
    b. they must follow local code guidelines as to materials used
    c. private systems must adhere to minimum separation distances for wells and septic systems
    d. if no local code guidelines are available, systems must comply with the New York Fire Prevention and Building code

129. The minimum electrical service installed in a residential home must be which of the following?
    a. 50 amps
    b. 100 amps
    c. 150 amps
    d. 200 amps

130. A device that melts and opens a circuit to stop electrical power when overheating occurs is called a:
    a. fuse
    b. distribution panel
    c. service drop
    d. voltameter

Construction and Environmental Issues
Part II Environmental Issues

131. Which of the following imposed stringent clean up standards and expanded the definition of those responsible for clean up?
    a. The National Environmental Policy Act
    b. State Environmental Quality Review Act
    c. the Clean Air Act
    d. Superfund Amendments and Reauthorization Act

132. The regulatory agency that oversees the safety of drinking water in New York is:
    a. Department of Environmental Conservation
    b. Department of Health
    c. Department of Agriculture
    d. Department of State

133. One of the biggest dangers in highly corrosive water is that it may contain large amounts of:
    a. radon
    b. PCBs
    c. lead
    d. CFCs

134. The regulatory agency that licenses individuals to apply termiticide in New York is the:
    a. Department of Environmental Conservation
    b. Department of Health
    c. Department of Parks
    d. Department of State

135. A fibrous mineral used in many construction applications such as ceiling tiles and roof shingles is called:
    a. lead
    b. asbestos
    c. radon
    d. UFFI

136. The Residential Lead-based Hazard Reduction Act calls for:
    a. a ban on the sale of all homes that contain lead paint
    b. homeowners to remove all lead paint before the property is put up for sale
    c. funding for homeowners to remove all lead paint from their home
    d. a mutually agreeable 10-day period for a lead paint assessment before a purchaser becomes obligated under a contract

137. Radon most generally enters the home:
    a. through openings in the attic or roof area
    b. when people leave their windows open for long periods of time
    c. when there is a heavy rainstorm
    d. through small cracks in the foundation wall

138. According to the EPA, which level of radon concentration is considered safe?
    a. no level
    b. more than 1 picocurie
    c. more than 2 picocuries
    d. more than 4 picocuries

139. If the indoor air quality of a commercial building causes large numbers of people to fall ill, this is called:
    a. an unhappy event
    b. sick building syndrome
    c. radon toxicity
    d. commercial building syndrome

140. A toxic liquid organic compound that was used as an insulating medium for electrical transformers and which has polluted both the soil and waterways in New York called:
    a. radon
    b. UFFI
    c. chlorofluorocarbons
    d. PCBs

Valuation Process and Pricing Properties

141. An analysis of the competition in the market place that a property will face upon sale attempts is called a(n):
    a. appraisal
    b. evaluation
    c. comparative market analysis
    d. cost approach to value

142. Which of the following methods are NOT used for appraisal purposes?
    a. income approach
    b. sales comparison approach
    c. cost approach
    d. comparative market analysis

143. An owner who uses a residential property for vacation purposes only may attribute which type of value to this property?
    a. assessed value
    b. insurance value
    c. value in use
    d. investment value

144. Which of the following is a value estimate of real property?
    a. appraisal of a single-family home
    b. feasibility studies
    c. highest and best use studies
    d. land utilization studies

145. A property will probably NOT sell for market value under which of the following conditions?
    a. buyer and seller are equally motivated
    b. a reasonable time is allowed for exposure in the market place
    c. the buyer and seller are related to each other
    d. it is an arms-length transaction

146. Which of the following regarding the price of a property is TRUE? Price:
    a. always equals cost
    b. is always more than the cost
    c. is always equivalent to the market value of a property
    d. is not always equivalent to the market value of a property

147. In the construction of a property, if time schedules are not met or other construction problems occur, which of the following would most likely apply? The:
    a. market value will equal the cost
    b. cost may exceed the market value
    c. cost will be below the market value
    d. price will definitely have to equal the cost

148. In the construction of a property, the cost of architectural and engineering fees are called:
    a. direct costs
    b. hard costs
    c. payment schedule
    d. indirect costs

149. Comparables used in the creation of a comparative market analysis should be:
    a. as similar as possible to the subject property
    b. exactly the same as the subject property
    c. as different as possible from the subject property
    d. located in a different neighborhood from the subject property

150. Which of the following is NOT an appropriate comparable for a comparative market analysis?
    a. expired listings
    b. current competing properties
    c. properties yet to be built
    d. sold properties

Human Rights and Fair Housing

151. Redlining is
    a. steering home seekers to a particular neighborhood
    b. drawing red circles on a zoning map indicating what areas are prime housing markets
    c. denying or restricting loans in a certain area by a lending institution
    d. a zoning procedure

152. The Civil Rights Act of 1866:
    a. prohibits all discrimination based on race
    b. prohibits discrimination in federally funded housing only
    c. allows an exception to racial discrimination for an owner occupied two-family dwelling
    d. does not apply to nonlicensed persons

153. Under the Federal Fair Housing Act, an administrative law judge may impose which of the following penalties for a "pattern of discrimination"?
    a. up to $10,000
    b. up to $50,000
    c. not more than $1 million
    d. the penalty is not limited by statute and may be determined by the court

154. Illegal blockbusting is described as:
    a. purchase of a home in a neighborhood by a member of a minority group
    b. directing home seekers into an area to change its character
    c. directing certain home seekers away from an area in order to maintain its character
    d. when homeowners are told by real estate salespeople that a member of a protected class is moving into their neighborhood, causing them to panic and place their homes for sale

155. What is illegal steering?
    a. leading prospective homeowners toward or away from certain areas
    b. refusing to make loans to persons in certain areas
    c. a requirement to join MLS
    d. a practice of fixing commission rates by an MLS steering committee

156. One of the differences between the federal Fair Housing Law and the New York Human Rights Law is that:
    a. the federal law does not cover rental housing
    b. the New York law does not have exemptions as in the federal law
    c. the New York law covers commercial property as well as residential
    d. the federal law lacks monetary penalties for violation

157. The Americans with Disabilities Act covers which of the following?
    a. single-family homes
    b. vacant land
    c. places of amusement only
    d. buildings open to the public as well as multi-family dwellings

158. In addition to federal law, protected classes under the New York Human Rights Law includes:
    a. familial status and race
    b. age and marital status
    c. race and religion
    d. disability and familial status

159. Nancy owns and lives in a duplex in Rochester, New York. She wishes to rent out the other apartment. Nancy:
    a. must rent her home to any person who is financially qualified
    b. may not discriminate against individuals because they are a certain race
    c. must rent her home to families with children, if approached
    d. must place her property for rent in a local newspaper if she does not use the services of a salesperson

160. An area designated by the Department of State where salesperson and brokers may not solicit listings is called a(n):
    a. cease and desist zone
    b. area under moratorium
    c. quarantined zone
    d. market allocation area

Real Estate Mathematics

161. A real estate broker earns a $12,500 commission in the sale of a condominium. His commission rate is 7%. What is the asking price of the condo? (Round off to the nearest dollar)
    a. $158,600
    b. $178,571
    c. $357,269
    d. $458,213

162. A broker earns a commission of $8,250. His commission rate is 7.5%. What is the selling price of the property?
    a. $80,000
    b. $90,000
    c. $100,000
    d. $110,000

163. A property valued at $475,000 appreciates 2% per year. How much is the property worth after two years?
    a. $484,500
    b. $493,175
    c. $494,190
    d. $501,160

164. An office space is 52 feet wide x 162 feet long and leases for $75,000 per year. What is the price per square foot?
    a. $8.90
    b. $15
    c. $20
    d. $25

165. An acre of land has a width of 425 feet. If this acre of land is rectangular in shape, what is its length?
    a. 85.5 feet
    b. 93 feet
    c. 102.5 feet
    d. 120 feet

166. The purchase price of a property is $175,000. The bank authorizes a loan-to-value ratio of 90%. What is the amount of the loan authorized?
    a. $90,000
    b. $100,000
    c. $125,000
    d. $157,500

167. A property closes on November 15. The yearly property taxes are $2,500. What is the credit to the seller on the closing statement?
    a. $256
    b. $312.50
    c. $375
    d. $476.89

168. A property sells for $120,000. The buyer obtains an 80% loan. If the bank charges 3 points at closing, how much in points must the buyer pay?
    a. $1,589
    b. $2,245
    c. $2,880
    d. $3,496

169. A loan of $50,000 is repaid in full one year after the loan is made. If the interest rate on the loan is 9.5%, what amount of interest is owned?
    a. $4,750
    b. $5,000
    c. $5,765
    d. $6,987

170. A property sells at the assessed value. The annual real property tax is $2,304 at a tax rate of $24 per thousand of tax value. The property is taxed at 80% of assessed value. What is the selling price?
    a. $110,000
    b. $120,000
    c. $130,000
    d. $140,000

Municipal Agencies

171. The legislative power of a city is vested in:
    a. the mayor
    b. its city council
    c. the state legislature
    d. zoning board of appeals

172. The main function of a city or town planning board is to advise on:
    a. environmental issues
    b. wetland regulation
    c. school policy
    d. land use matters

173. Which of the following government agencies may grant a variance?
    a. citizen's advisory council
    b. town board
    c. zoning board of appeals
    d. planning board

174. Xavier is seeking information about constructing a property near a wetland. He can find information and guidance from which of the following?
    a. conservation advisory council
    b. architectural review board
    c. zoning board of appeals
    d. county legislature

175. Building departments CANNOT perform which of the following:
    a. issue building permits
    b. issue certificates of occupancies
    c. inspect ongoing construction
    d. rule on variance applications

176. The document containing each property's assessment in a municipality is the:
    a. title register
    b. city or town budget
    c. assessment roll
    d. tax map

177. In some cities and towns, the official or agency that collects fees for water usage and other permits is the:
    a. tax assessor
    b. receiver of taxes
    c. engineer
    d. building department

178. The New York state agency that oversees wetland regulations is the:
    a. Department of Environmental Conservation
    b. Department of Health
    c. Department of Public Works
    d. Department of State

179. A town or village planning board consists of how many members?
    a. two to four
    b. five to seven
    c. seven to nine
    d. any numbers as decided by the town board or village board of trustees

180. Meri wants more information about renovating a historic property. Which agency would be LEAST likely to be involved in this process?
    a. historic preservation commission
    b. zoning board of appeals
    c. building department
    d. conservation advisory council

Property Insurance

181. A clause in an insurance policy that modifies or changes the insurance policy in some way is known as a (n):
    a. endorsement
    b. peril
    c. deductible
    d. umbrella

182. Insurance obtained through the New York Property Insurance Underwriting Association can be undesirable because:
    a. it is unreliable
    b. the premiums are higher than those obtained through the voluntary market
    c. only certain areas of New York are insured
    d. there is a long waiting list

183. The National Flood Insurance Program is administered by:
    a. the NYS Insurance Department
    b. FEMA
    c. HUD
    d. the Army Corps of Engineers

184. According to New York law, which of the following deductibles must be disclosed to the insured?
    a. personal property
    b. fire
    c. flood
    d. windstorm

185. As long as the insurance company states the reason for the cancellation, an insurance policy may be cancelled within how many days?
    a. 25
    b. 30
    c. 60
    d. 90

186. The cost of a homeowners policy is directly related to which of the following:
    a. the policy holder only
    b. the property only
    c. a statewide fee schedule
    d. both a and b

187. The amount the insured must pay towards a claim before receiving any policy benefits is called the:
    a. premium
    b. peril
    c. deductible
    d. endorsement

188. An excess liability policy, providing additional coverage above that offered by primary policies is called a (n):
    a. replacement cost premium
    b. umbrella policy
    c. luxury coverage
    d. homeowners special form policy

189. In the insurance policy contract, the basic coverage is outlined in which part of the policy?
    a. declarations page
    b. actual cost section
    c. contingency plan endorsement section
    d. statement of liability

190. Which of the following is NOT a type of coverage in an insurance policy?
    a. dwelling
    b. personal property
    c. loss of use
    d. functional obsolescence

Taxes and Assessments

191. Which of the following is an example of a property that is NOT tax exempt?
    a. VA hospital
    b. synagogue
    c. gas station
    d. state office building

192. The tax rate is determined by:
    a. the city or town council
    b. the assessor
    c. the amount of the tax levy
    d. the census

193. The percentage at which properties are assessed in a locality is called the:
    a. tax levy
    b. level of assessment
    c. residential assessment ratio
    d. tax rate

194. Reassessments can be performed on properties:
    a. when improvements are made only
    b. on a regular prescribed basis only
    c. as a random spot check on any property in the locality
    d. both a and b

195. Which of the following CANNOT collect real property taxes in New York?
    a. cities
    b. towns
    c. villages
    d. the state

196. Which of the following CANNOT receive an exemption from paying real property taxes?
    a. those with disabilities
    b. property owners under 25 years old
    c. seniors
    d. veterans

197. The purpose of the board of assessment review is to:
    a. levy taxes
    b. set uniform percentages
    c. develop the equalization rate
    d. hear grievances

198. If a property owner believes that his property's assessed value is greater than the property's full value, he may claim that he has been subject to:
    a. unequal assessment
    b. excessive assessment
    c. unlawful assessment
    d. misclassification

199. A judicial review of a tax protest in the New York Supreme Court is called a (n)
    a. tax certiorari proceeding
    b. grievance
    c. Article 78 proceeding
    d. tax hearing

200. The first task in determining the assessment for tax purposes is to:
    a. hold a referendum to decide who is exempt
    b. evaluate the zoning regulations for the community
    c. establish the market value of each parcel of land within the taxing unit
    d. file a petition of appeal

Condominiums and Cooperatives

201. Ownership in a cooperative is evidenced by:
    a. shares of stock
    b. a deed
    c. a recognition agreement
    d. an alteration agreement

202. The type of ownership interest that a cooperative owner has in his real property is:
    a. freehold
    b. leasehold
    c. fee simple absolute
    d. tenant at will

203. Which of the following is NOT included in a condominium offering plan?
    a. initial declaration
    b. prospectus
    c. initial price of the units
    d. proprietary lease

204. With regard to a condominium or cooperative, whether or not a tenant can advertise from their apartment window, is included in the:
    a. alteration agreement
    b. house rules
    c. recognition agreement
    d. letter of intent

205. A board package, submitted to the cooperative board of directors, consists mainly of:
    a. societal status information
    b. family history
    c. financial data
    d. reasons for purchase

206. An agreement that outlines the responsibilities between the cooperative corporation and the lender is called a (n):
    a. CSP1 statement
    b. subordination agreement
    c. alteration agreement
    d. recognition agreement

207. Which of the following characterizes a condop?
    a. a cooperative that does not have board interviews
    b. a building that has both condominium and cooperative ownership
    c. a condominium that has no board of directors
    d. a condominium or cooperative that does not have an offering plan adopted by the attorney general

208. Pet restrictions, repair obligations, and use of the common elements are disclosed in a condominium's:
    a. bylaws
    b. letter of intent
    c. CPS1 statement
    d. tenant declaration

209. During the CPS1 period or phase, which of the following is TRUE in the marketing of condominiums or cooperatives?
    a. the developer need not following any attorney general rules governing advertising
    b. only the attorney general can set the price for the units
    c. the developer may set the market price for the units
    d. no firm price can be declared by the developer for individual units

210. Which of the following is TRUE regarding the mansion tax? The tax:
    a. applies to all residential properties sold for $1 million or more
    b. applies only to condominiums and cooperatives when the units are over 5000 square feet
    c. applies to one-, two-, and three-unit residential properties as well as condominiums and cooperatives sold for $1 million or more
    d. only applies in New York City

Commercial and Investment Real Estate

211. Which of the following is a benefit that depreciation provides?
     a. tax credit
     b. tax deduction
     c. tax evasion
     d. tax basis

212. Which of the following is NOT a tax deductible expense for a business property?
     a. advertising
     b. utilities
     c. mortgage principal
     d. insurance

213. An investor purchases a $2,000,000 multi-family apartment complex with a $500,000 down payment. Each month, the cash flow from rentals, less expenses, is $15,000. What is the cash-on-cash return?
     a. 28 percent
     b. 31 percent
     c. 36 percent
     d. 42 percent

214. The value of an income property is $850,000 and the capitalization rate is 12%. What is the projected annual net income?
     a. $82,500
     b. $87,000
     c. $98,000
     d. $102,000

215. When offering available square footage to tenants, property owners generally charge for which of the following:
     a. usable square footage
     b. rentable square footage
     c. carpetable area
     d. effective square footage

216. Which of the following defines when an investment will generate a positive return?
     a. attornment
     b. expense stop
     c. point of no return
     d. natural breakeven point

217. A lease clause that states that the landlord's lender and future owners of the building cannot terminate the lease as long as the tenant fulfills lease obligations is called a (n):
     a. escalation clause
     b. estoppel
     c. subordination clause
     d. nondisturbance clause

218. Which of the following is a type of lease escalation clause?
     a. Porter's wage formula
     b. estoppel
     c. use clause
     d. subordination

219. Generally, with a real estate investment, the greater the risk of loss, which of the following is TRUE?
     a. the greater the return on investment
     b. the less the return on investment
     c. risk has nothing to do with return
     d. risk and return are always equal

220. The use of OPM, or other people's money, describes which investment concept?
     a. risk
     b. return
     c. leverage
     d. debt service

Income Tax Issues in Real Estate

221. According to IRS rules, real property taxes are deductible for which of the following?
     a. a personal residence
     b. a second home
     c. an inherited property
     d. all of the above

222. If a taxpayer's tax rate is above the 15% income bracket and he has held a property for longer than 12 months, when he sells the property, he will be taxed at a rate of:
     a. 5 percent
     b. 10 percent
     c. 15 percent
     d. 20 percent

223. Petros lost $15,000 of his personal funds in the stock market in the taxable year 2008. Under what circumstances can he deduct this amount from his yearly income taxes?
a. only if he earned under $25,000 for 2008
b. only if he is in the 15 percent tax bracket
c. only if he is unemployed
d. under no circumstances

224. Property eligible for a tax-deferred exchange does NOT include which of the following?
a. industrial property
b. commercial property
c. a personal residence
d. a hotel or motel

225. Which of the following may be deducted on a real property purchaser's income tax return under certain conditions?
a. appraisal fees
b. points
c. notary fees
d. preparation fee for the mortgage

226. The main housing credit agency in New York is which of the following? The:
a. NYS Division of Housing and Community Renewal
b. HUD
c. FEMA
d. NYS Division of Human Rights

227. In reference to the straight-line method for depreciating nonresidential property, it may be depreciated over how many years?
a. 15 years
b. 27.5 years
c. 35.5 years
d. 39 years

228. Which IRS rule allows first-time homebuyers to use IRA distributions to fund up to $10,000 of their new home cost without paying an early distribution penalty?
a. rule of four
b. age 59 1/2 rule
c. safe harbor law
d. IRA exemption clause

229. How many days from the day of closing does a real estate exchangor have to contract for another (replacement) property?
a. 15 days
b. 30 days
c. 45 days
d. 60 days

230. In a tax-deferred exchange, any cash in the exchange is called the:
a. equity
b. collateral
c. cache
d. boot

Mortgage Brokerage

231. The New York agency that registers mortgage brokers is which of the following?
a. Banking Department
b. Insurance Department
c. Department of State
d. Attorney General's Office

232. Which of the following describes the experience requirement for a NYS licensed real estate broker to obtain a mortgage broker license?
a. one year in the mortgage business
b. two years in the mortgage business
c. a current real estate broker's license
d. a real estate salesperson who has been licensed for at least one year

233. A mortgage broker who represents a purchaser in negotiating a mortgage loan is which of the following?
a. agent
b. intermediary
c. facilitator
d. none of the above

234. A mortgage broker who represents the purchasers in negotiating a mortgage while also representing the sellers as a real estate broker in the same transaction is acting as a (n):
a. general agent
b. facilitator
c. dual agent
d. single agent

235. The minimum line of credit required to be registered in New York as a mortgage banker is:
a. $250,000
b. $500,000
c. $1 million
d. $2 million

236. Which of the following involve verifying a purchaser's credit and employment history?
a. appraisal
b. validation
c. pre approval
d. statement of net worth

237. A request by a purchaser to reserve a certain loan interest rate for a specified time is called a (n):
a. rate lock
b. commitment
c. rate cap
d. interest reserve

238. The process in which the lender evaluates all of the borrower's financial data and determines if the borrower will obtain the loan is called:
a. alienation
b. pre approval
c. clarification
d. loan underwriting

239. A lender's rebate is payment to which of the following?
a. loan underwriter
b. seller
c. purchaser
d. mortgage broker

240. A loan that does NOT meet the Federal Reserve Bank loan criteria for funding is known as:
a. illegal
b. secondary
c. nonconforming
d. straight term

Property Management

241. If a property manager works for one owner, which of the following is TRUE? He:
a. must have a broker license
b. must have a minimum of a salesperson license
c. does not need a real estate license
d. is always an independent contractor

242. Which of the following creates an agency relationship between the property manager and the owner?
a. management agreement
b. management proposal
c. listing agreement
d. letter of intent

243. In managing a property, risk management has to do with:
a. financial risk
b. liability when the public enters the property
c. managing the activities of employees
d. tenant behavior

244. If a building is 98 percent occupied, the property manager may feel justified in:
a. believing that the laws of supply and demand are not in favor of the property
b. rewriting the leases during the lease term
c. lowering the rents
d. raising the rents

245. Property income and expenses for week-to-week operations are computed in which type of budget?
a. cash flow
b. capital reserve
c. stabilized
d. operating

246. Randy rents out six apartments in his building for $750 per month and seven apartments for $1,050 per month. Figuring in a 5% vacancy rate, what is the annual projected rent roll?
a. $135,090
b. $139,500
c. $142,200
d. $185,300

247. Which document prepared by a property
manager relates expense items to the
operating budget for the period?
a. property management agreement
b. property management report
c. rent roll
d. stabilized budget

248. Lydia, a property manager, enlisted her
maintenance team to go through the
building and assess and repair all items that
may need repair or replacement for the
calendar year. This is an example of:
a. excessive oversight
b. due diligence
c. preventative maintenance
d. corrective maintenance

249. In New York if a property manager works
for one owner, which of the following is
required? A (n):
a. real estate broker license
b. BOMI affiliation
c. IREM designation
d. none of the above

250. In her position as managing agent for a
small apartment complex, Alexa, a real
estate broker, accepts a small bonus from
the landscapers since she hired them to
maintain the complex. Alexa does not tell
the owners about the bonus. Which of the
following is TRUE? Alexa:
a. is violating her fiduciary duty to the
owners
b. may accept the bonus
c. may be illegally accepting payment
d. both a and c

Sample Practice Licensing Exams

The following two exams, Practice Exams 1 and 2 are formatted to match the New York State licensing exam. That is, the topics, and the number of questions for each topic is similar to that of the actual test. The total number of exam questions, 75, are the same number as the state licensing exam. Because the practice exams are weighted to match the actual test, your performance on these should be a good indicator of your performance on the state exam.

Tear out the Answer Sheet on the next pages, and use it to record your responses You may want to photocopy the blank answer sheet so that you can use it a second time.

Complete the practice exams under exam conditions-find a quiet place and allow 1.5 uninterrupted hours for each exam. This is the same amount of time allotted to the state exam. After completing the exam, check your answers with the "Answer Key for Practice Exams" at the back of this guide. Review all incorrect answers. The rationale for the correct answer appears in the Answer Key. For a complete study experience, use the references in the Answer Key to review the related material in the textbook, *New York Real Estate for Salespersons, 4*[th] *e.*

Practice Exam 1

1. _____	21. _____	41. _____	71. _____
2. _____	22. _____	42. _____	72. _____
3. _____	23. _____	43. _____	73. _____
4. _____	24. _____	44. _____	74. _____
5. _____	25. _____	45. _____	75. _____
6. _____	26. _____	46. _____	
7. _____	27. _____	47. _____	
8. _____	28. _____	48. _____	
9. _____	29. _____	49. _____	
10. _____	30. _____	50. _____	
11. _____	31. _____	51. _____	
12. _____	32. _____	52. _____	
13. _____	33. _____	53. _____	
14. _____	34. _____	54. _____	
15. _____	35. _____	55. _____	
16. _____	36. _____	56. _____	
17. _____	37. _____	57. _____	
18. _____	38. _____	58. _____	
19. _____	39. _____	59. _____	
20. _____	40. _____	60. _____	

Practice Exam 2

1. _____	21. _____	41. _____	71. _____
2. _____	22. _____	42. _____	72. _____
3. _____	23. _____	43. _____	73. _____
4. _____	24. _____	44. _____	74. _____
5. _____	25. _____	45. _____	75. _____
6. _____	26. _____	46. _____	
7. _____	27. _____	47. _____	
8. _____	28. _____	48. _____	
9. _____	29. _____	49. _____	
10. _____	30. _____	50. _____	
11. _____	31. _____	51. _____	
12. _____	32. _____	52. _____	
13. _____	33. _____	53. _____	
14. _____	34. _____	54. _____	
15. _____	35. _____	55. _____	
16. _____	36. _____	56. _____	
17. _____	37. _____	57. _____	
18. _____	38. _____	58. _____	
19. _____	39. _____	59. _____	
20. _____	40. _____	60. _____	

Practice Exam I

License Law and Regulations (3 hours) (3 questions)

1. The license term for real estate salespersons and brokers is:
   a. one year
   b. two years
   c. three years
   d. four years

2. A salesperson may receive compensation from:
   a. his client
   b. his principal
   c. his sponsoring broker
   d. any licensed broker

3. A salesperson may draw legal documents:
   a. with permission of her sponsoring broker only
   b. under no circumstances
   c. with permission of the principal
   d. if the salesperson has a notary public license

Law of Agency including Independent Contractor (11 hours) (11 questions)

4. If the parties to a residential real estate transaction agree to dual agency representation:
   a. all confidential information given to the agent by the seller or buyer must be disclosed to both parties
   b. both seller and buyer must pay a full commission to the agent
   c. both seller and purchaser forfeit the right to undivided loyalty by the agent
   d. DOS must be informed of the agreement

5. Which of the following is an illegal type of payment arrangement for brokers?
   a. percentage of final sales price
   b. flat fee
   c. commission schedule set forth by the local board of REALTORS®
   d. referral fee

6. Belinda, a salesperson, works for Broker Barry and in that capacity has received informed consent from a seller to represent him in the sale of his home. What is Belinda's relationship to this seller/principal?
   a. broker's agent
   b. dual agent
   c. subagent
   d. buyer agent

7. In a buyer agency relationship, the buyer is the:
   a. customer
   b. principal
   c. subagent
   d. third party

8. The disclosure form for one- to four-unit residential properties is required in which of the following circumstances:
   a. at the time that a seller enters into a listing agreement with a broker
   b. when prospects enter an open house
   c. when prospects call to inquire about a property
   d. at the closing

9. Belle Properties Brokerage and Ruby Real Estate decided that, since they were the only two companies that offered residential property for sale in a small town, they would both charge the same commission rate. These two firms are guilty of:
   a. nothing at all
   b. an illegal group boycott
   c. illegal price fixing
   d. an illegal market allocation agreement

10. In a dual agency situation within a brokerage firm, with disclosure and informed consent, one agent can represent the buyer and one the seller. Both of these agents are called:
    a. designated agents
    b. listing agents
    c. mandatory agents
    d. broker's agents

11. The sellers tell Carlos, a real estate agent, that the basement of their house floods every spring. The sellers do not wish to disclose this information. What should Carlos do?
    a. agree with his sellers
    b. inform his sellers that this information must be disclosed
    c. obtain a signed release from the sellers so that Agent Carlos is not liable should there be a lawsuit
    d. refuse to take a listing since the property has a material defect

12. What do subagents, listing agents, seller agents, and single agents have in common? They:
    a. are all dual agents
    b. all represent the seller
    c. all must belong to the multiple listing service
    d. are all cooperating agents

13. If a salesperson is NOT paid according to hours worked, the salesperson is most likely classified by IRS as a(n):
    a. common law employee
    b. statutory employee
    c. independent contractor
    d. sales associate

14. Regulations governing the status of employees or independent contractors are determined by:
    a. the broker
    b. New York State Association of Realtors
    c. federal and state statutes
    d. Department of State

Legal Issues
Estates and Interests (3 hours) (3 questions)

15. Mike and Mindy held title to a property together with no right of survivorship. They most likely held the property:
    a. as joint tenants
    b. as tenants in common
    c. in severalty
    d. as joint tenants by the entirety

16. Which of the following water rights belong to an owner of property bordering a flowing body of water?
    a. subsurface rights
    b. riparian rights
    c. chattel rights
    d. bundle of rights

17. Juan plans to sell some household furnishings when he sells his house. He will most likely use a document called a (n):
    a. sales contract
    b. bill of sale
    c. transfer affidavit
    d. purchase offer

Legal Issues
Liens and Easements (2.5 hours) (3 questions)

18. Real property taxes are examples of:
    a. voluntary specific liens
    b. involuntary specific liens
    c. voluntary general liens
    d. involuntary general liens

19. A lien filed by an individual who provides labor to a property and is NOT paid is called a:
    a. lis pendens
    b. subordination lien
    c. mechanic's lien
    d. real property judgment

20. Goldie allows her neighbor, Mattie, to use a path on her property to access the lakefront. Which of the following is TRUE?
    a. Goldie's property is the servient tenement
    b. this is an encroachment
    c. this is a type of lien
    d. this is type of grant

Legal Issues
Deeds (2.5 hours) (3 questions)

21. For a deed to be eligible for recording, it must have which of the following? A(n):
    a. metes and bounds description
    b. habendum clause
    c. acknowledgment
    d. covenant of warranty

22. Which of the following is NOT a judicial deed?
    a. executor's deed
    b. guardian's deed
    c. sheriff's deed
    d. Torren's certificate

Legal Issues
Title Closing and Costs (2 hours) (2 questions)

23. The seller will accept a purchase money mortgage from the buyer. On the closing statement, this amount appears as a:
    a. seller debit
    b. seller credit
    c. buyer debit
    d. balancing disbursement

24. Which of the following is NOT generally a purchaser closing cost?
    a. title insurance policy
    b. mortgage recording tax
    c. discount points
    d. delinquent real property taxes

The Contract of Sale and Leases
Leases (1 hour) (1 question)

25. Amy transferred her lease contract to her friend, Jamie. Jamie will now have to make the lease payments to the landlord. Which of the following has taken place? A(n):
    a. assignment
    b. sublease
    c. constructive eviction
    d. holdover tenancy

The Contract of Sale and Leases
Contracts (1 hour) (2 questions)

26. A court ordered Nancy to pay Tessie $10,000 because she did not purchase Tessie's property even though they had a valid contract. This monetary payment is called:
    a. specific performance
    b. rescission
    c. liquidated damages
    d. novation

The Contract of Sale and Leases
Contract Preparation (1 hour) (1 question)

27. In order for a real estate salesperson to prepare a fill-in-the-blanks contract of sale approved by the Board of Realtors, the contract must:
    a. be less than three pages
    b. be clearly captioned and easy to understand
    c. have an attorney review clause
    d. notarized

Real Estate Finance (5 hours) (5 questions)

28. Which type of mortgage loan requires, for example, monthly payments of $1,200 for 15 years and a final payment of $10,000?
    a. graduated payment mortgage
    b. flexible payment mortgage
    c. wraparound mortgage
    d. balloon mortgage

29. Up to the time a foreclosure sale is held, a borrower who has defaulted on his loan may be able to regain his property by paying the outstanding debt. This is a (n):
    a. deed in lieu of foreclosure
    b. equity of redemption
    c. deficiency judgment
    d. recovery grace period

30. The clause in a mortgage stating that a lender may declare the entire balance due if the borrower is in default is called the:
    a. prepayment penalty clause
    b. granting clause
    c. acceleration clause
    d. defeasance clause

31. In which type of mortgage are two or more parcels of real estate pledged as security for a mortgage debt?
    a. package mortgage
    b. blanket mortgage
    c. bridge loan
    d. installment land contract

32. An agency of HUD that insures loans to protect lenders against financial loss is:
    a. Fannie Mae
    b. Sonny Mae
    c. FHA
    d. Freddie Mac

Land Use Regulations (3 hours) (3 questions)

33. The New York law regulating the sale of unimproved lots across state lines is called:
    a. the Interstate Land Sales Full Disclosure Act
    b. Article 9-A of the Real Property Law
    c. the State Environmental Quality Review Act
    d. the Uniform Fire Prevention and Building Code

34. The taking of property under the government's right of eminent domain is called:
    a. escheat
    b. estoppel
    c. in rem
    d. condemnation

35. Emma wishes to add another story to her home; however, the new height would not comply with the current zoning ordinance. She would need to apply for a(n):
    a. nonconforming use
    b. use variance
    c. area variance
    d. spot zone

Construction and Environmental Issues (5 hours) (5 questions)

36. The foundation walls of a property are usually composed of:
    a. concrete
    b. wood
    c. steel
    d. iron

37. The area under the roof extension is called the:
    a. frieze board
    b. fascia
    c. soffit
    d. sheathing

38. For residential one- and two-family properties in New York, and condominiums and cooperatives, which of the following is required at closing?
    a. smoke alarm affidavit
    b. carbon monoxide detector affidavit
    c. agency disclosure
    d. both a and b

39. The New York law that requires preparation of an environmental impact statement on properties that a government body has the jurisdiction to review is the:
    a. Superfund Amendment
    b. State Environmental Quality Review Act
    c. Real Estate Settlement Procedures Act
    d. Comprehensive Environmental Response, Compensation and Liability Act (CERCLA)

40. Sales contracts used for target properties under the Residential Lead-Based Hazard Reduction Act must include:
    a. nothing different than before the law was enacted
    b. specific disclosure and acknowledgment language
    c. approval by an agent of HUD
    d. an attachment indicating the exact age of the property

Valuation Process and Pricing Properties (3 hours) (3 questions)

41. The appraisal approach most similar to a comparative market analysis is the:
    a. income approach
    b. cost approach
    c. capitalization approach
    d. sales comparison approach

42. A land utilization study that does not necessarily produce an estimate of value can be best defined as a(n):
    a. evaluation
    b. appraisal
    c. comparative market analysis
    d. value in use

43. One of the most important aspects of marketing a property is:
    a. pricing the property at the lowest possible price to make sure of a timely sale
    b. knowing the competition and adjusting pricing and marketing strategies accordingly
    c. ignoring the competition and allowing the property to sell based on its own merits
    d. effecting a sale within 18 months of the listing date

Human Rights and Fair Housing (4 hours) (4 questions)

44. Individuals who visit real estate offices posing as prospective home seekers to see if race influences the buying process are called:
    a. civil rights inspectors
    b. real estate licensees
    c. testers
    d. inspectors

45. The owner of a single-family property in Syosset, Long Island asks a salesperson to find a "nice couple without children" to purchase their home. The broker:
    a. may take this listing because the property owner has the right to specify who purchases his property
    b. may take the listing but must ask for a written statement from the owner to cover any iability problems
    c. may take the listing only with permission of her supervising broker
    d. must refuse this listing

46. The term *blockbusting* refers to:
    a. phone calls soliciting prospective buyers or sellers in a cease and desist zone
    b. offering property for sale only to persons of a certain race
    c. prompting homeowners to sell their properties due to the entry of certain persons of a particular race or religion into the neighborhood
    d. the government's right of eminent domain to condemn and destroy older vacant buildings in a neighborhood

47. The lending department of Money Bank decided not to make home improvement loans to residents of Lonely Heights because a survey completed by the bank showed a higher number of single- parent families living in that neighborhood. Money Bank is guilty of:
    a. redlining
    b. steering
    c. nothing at all
    d. blockbusting

Real Estate Mathematics (1 hour) (2 questions)

48. A real estate salesperson sells a property for $90,000. The commission on this sale to the real estate firm with whom the salesperson is associated is 6%. The salesperson receives 60% of the total commission paid to the real estate firm. What is the firm's share of the commission in dollars?
    a. $2,450
    b. $3.240
    c. $4,500
    d. $4,750

49. If the assessed value of a property is $217,500 and the tax value is 100% of the assessed value, what is the annual tax if the rate is $2.00 per $100?
    a. $2,450
    b. $3,500
    c. $3,475
    d. $4,350

Municipal Agencies (2 hours) (2 questions)

50. A municipal agency is given the job of mapping a large parcel of land that was granted to the city. Which state agency would most probably be the lead agency for this project?
    a. assessor's office
    b. zoning board of appeals
    c. planning board
    d. architectural review board

51. A town on Long Island does not allow any buildings higher than four stories. Francesca wants to add two more floors to her two-story building. Which agencies might be involved in reviewing her construction application?
    a. zoning board of appeals
    b. architectural review board
    c. conservation advisory council
    d. both a and b

Property Insurance (2 hours) (2 questions)

52. The Kelly's had $2,500 worth of damage to their house when a tree fell through the front window during a storm. They received a payment of $1,500 from the insurance company. Which term explains the missing $1,000?
    a. peril
    b. deductible
    c. umbrella
    d. endorsement

53. The Lee's damaged their oven in a small kitchen fire and were reimbursed for the actual cost of replacing the oven. This means that their coverage was:
    a. for actual cash value
    b. for replacement cost
    c. for personal liability
    d. an umbrella policy

Taxes and Assessments (3 hours) (3 questions)

54. A type of map, drawn to scale, showing all of the property parcels with a city, town, or village, and their size shape and dimensions is called a (n):
    a. plat
    b. blueprint
    c. survey
    d. tax map

55. A property taxing unit may be a (n):
    a. city
    b. town
    c. county
    d. all of the above

56. Municipalities use residential assessment ratios:
    a. for revaluation projects
    b. if there are less than five residential sales that year
    c. for board of assessment review grievances
    d. to determine tax exemptions

Condominiums and Cooperatives (4 hours) (3 questions)

57. Which of the following is FALSE regarding a cooperative?
    a. it is a non for profit corporation
    b. it is formed for the benefit of its members
    c. it is owned by the cooperative cooperation
    d. a unit owner receives a deed to his individual unit

58. The owner or developer of a condominium or cooperative is called the:
    a. director
    b. sponsor
    c. trustor
    d. originator

59. The New York Attorney General's rules for testing the market for a new condominium or cooperative development are contained in:
    a. the UCC-1 statement
    b. the CPS1 statement
    c. Civil Practice Rules and Procedure
    d. Section 443 of the Real Property Law

Commercial and Investment Properties (10 hours) (9 questions)

60. An operating statement adjusted to reflect a potential change in income and expenses based upon the investor's knowledge of the real estate market is called a (n):
    a. cash flow statement
    b. operating statement
    c. statement of net worth
    d. proforma statement

61. The net monthly income of a seven-unit apartment building is $2,250. The capitalization rate the lender uses is 7%. What is the value of the building?
    a. $299,010
    b. $385,714
    c. $410,926
    d. $450,509

62. A process that calculates the value of an asset in the past, present, and future is called:
    a. leverage
    b. the time value of money
    c. debt service
    d. net operating income

63. If a business property has an asset value of $1,000,000 with a debt of $750,000, what is the debt ratio?
    a. 50 percent
    b. 60 percent
    c. 75 percent
    d. 90 percent

64. Land is a more risky type of real estate investment for all of the following reasons EXCEPT:
    a. it may be more difficult to obtain financing
    b. there are no improvements on it
    c. it cannot be depreciated for tax purposes
    d. it always has less resale value than other types of property

65. Income received on a property without deducting expenses is called:
    a. NOI
    b. gross income
    c. net income
    d. debt service

66. The net proceeds or cash remaining after all expenses and debt services are paid is called:
    a. tax shelter
    b. gross income
    c. cash flow
    d. cash-on-cash return

67. The ratio of annual before-tax cash flow to the total amount of cash invested, expressed as a percentage is called the:
    a. capitalization rate
    b. rate of return
    c. income expense ratio
    d. cash=on-cash return

68. Investment in commercial real estate does NOT provide which of the following?
    a. deductible expenses
    b. income shelters
    c. depreciation allowances
    d. guaranteed profit over time

Income Tax Issues in Real Estate Transactions (3 hours) (3 questions)

69. Which of the following is NOT a tax bracket for federal income tax purposes?
    a. 15 percent
    b. 25 percent
    c. 28 percent
    d. 39 percent

70. Which of the following items are allowed federal tax deductions on home ownership?
    a. interest
    b. principal
    c. property taxes
    d. both a and c

71. Annie and Xavier, a married couple, bought their house five years ago for $350,000. They are in the 35 percent tax bracket. They recently sold it for $400,000. What is the amount of capital gains tax they must pay when they file their tax return?
    a. $2500
    b. $7,500
    c. $50,000
    d. no capital gains tax

Mortgage Brokerage (1 hour) (2 questions)

72. If an individual holds a real estate broker's license and wants to apply for a mortgage broker license, which of the following documents must be submitted to the Banking Department with his mortgage broker application?
    a. dual agency affidavit
    b. estoppel certificate
    c. fee application
    d. lender certification

73. Should a real estate salesperson want a mortgage broker license, what is the experience required?
    a. real estate salespersons do not need other experience to become a mortgage broker
    b. one year experience in the mortgage business
    c. two years experience in the mortgage business
    d. one year experience managing a real estate brokerage office

Property Management (2 hours) (2 questions)

74. Advisors to property managers who focus on long-term financial planning rather than day-to-day operations of the property are:
    a. real estate gurus
    b. resident managers
    c. financial advisors
    d. asset managers

75. A document submitted to the property owner outlining the commitment of the property owner once the manager is employed is the:
    a. management agreement
    b. management proposal
    c. property projection
    d. operating expense analysis

Practice Exam II

License Law and Regulations (3 hours) (3 questions)

1. To be licensed as a real estate broker, an individual must be at least how old?
   a. 16
   b. 18
   c. 20
   d. 21

2. Which of the following individuals is exempt from licensure?
   a. attorneys admitted to practice in the New York courts
   b. property managers who manage property for more than one individual or company
   c. individuals who only list property for sale
   d. auctioneers who only auction commercial real estate

3. To save on paperwork, Broker Bright decides to combine her office operating account with the deposits obtained from contracts of sale. Broker Bright is guilty of:
   a. nothing at all
   b. illegal commingling of funds
   c. an unauthorized practice of law
   d. accepting money without authorization

Law of Agency including Independent Contractor (11 hours) (11 questions)

4. A net listing is one:
   a. that requires the broker to have a fixed price for the property
   b. that is legal in New York
   c. that most brokers would prefer
   d. in which the seller specifies a certain amount of money to be received upon sale of the property and all monies above that amount are the broker's commission

5. A broker's agent is hired by the:
   a. principal
   b. seller
   c. customer
   d. broker

6. Which of the following is TRUE regarding dual agency relationships in New York?
   a. they are permissible with timely disclosure and informed consent
   b. they are illegal under all circumstances
   c. they are allowed only in commercial transactions
   d. they are allowed only in the sale of condominium or cooperative properties

7. A listing agreement in which the property is listed with only one broker who is entitled to a commission if he sells the property but not if the owner sells the property is called a(n):
   a. exclusive-right-to-sell agreement
   b. open listing agreement
   c. net listing agreement
   d. exclusive agency agreement

8. The first law to address antitrust violations was the:
   a. Clayton Antitrust Act
   b. Real Estate Settlement Procedures Act
   c. Sherman Antitrust Act
   d. New York Real Property Law

9. Sell-It-Today Brokerage requires that purchasers of its listed property apply for a mortgage with EZ Money Mortgage Company. This practice is:
   a. perfectly acceptable
   b. an example of an illegal tie-in arrangement
   c. an example of an illegal group boycott
   d. an example of an illegal market allocation agreement

10. An agency relationship created by an oral or written agreement between principal and agent is a (n):
    a. implied agency
    b. express agency
    c. dual agency
    d. power of attorney

11. Martin signs an exclusive-right-to-sell listing agreement for six months with Broker Gerald. Within one month, Martin sells his house himself and refuses to pay a commission to Gerald. Martin's behavior is a possible:
    a. reformation
    b. breach of contract
    c. injunction
    d. assignment

12. In a brokerage firm, the listing contracts are typically owned by the:
    a. salesperson who lists the property
    b. multiple listing service together with the brokerage firm
    c. principals who engaged the firm to market their properties
    d. brokerage firm

13. Which of the following activities is NOT an element of an independent contractor relationship?
    a. no compensation for specific number of hours worked
    b. salespersons can work any hours they choose
    c. commissions are paid with deductions for income taxes
    d. either the salesperson or broker may terminate the relationship at any time

14. Real estate licensees are classified as independent contractors under which of the following?
    a. Section 3508 (a) (b) of the IRS Code
    b. common law
    c. Article 12-A of the Real Property Law
    d. Section 443 of the Real Property Law

Legal Issues
Estates and Interests (3 hours) (3 questions)

15. Which of the following is NOT one of the four unities required for joint tenancy?
    a. unity of time
    b. unity of interest
    c. unity of partition
    d. unity of possession

16. Francois and Helena purchase a property and their attorney tells them that their title offers them the most complete form of ownership. Their ownership right is:
    a. fee simple on condition
    b. fee simple absolute
    c. fee simple defeasible
    d. a life estate

17. Kelly's mother deeds Kelly her beach house for Kelly's lifetime. Then the property goes to the A.S.P.C.A in memory of mother's favorite cat upon daughter Kelly's death. This is an example of a:
    a. fee simple absolute
    b. leasehold
    c. joint tenancy
    d. life estate

Legal Issues
Liens and Easements (2.5 hours) (2 questions)

18. A judgment is an example of a(n):
    a. voluntary specific lien
    b. involuntary specific lien
    c. voluntary general lien
    d. involuntary general lien

19. A legal notice that a lawsuit is pending concerning title to a particular property is called a(n):
    a. injunction
    b. lis pendens
    c. judgment
    d. mechanic's lien

20. Lionel buys a cabin in a remote area and has no road access except through his neighbor's adjoining property. Lionel's property requires a (n):
    a. easement by condemnation
    b. negative easement
    c. easement by necessity
    d. encroachment

Legal Issues
Deeds (2.5 hours) (2 questions)

21. A type of deed used in bankruptcy proceedings and foreclosures is a(n):
    a. sheriff's deed
    b. executor's deed
    c. referee's deed
    d. guardian's deed

22. In order to claim title by adverse possession in New York, the use must be open and notorious for how many years?
    a. 5
    b. 10
    c. 15
    d. 20

Title Closing and Costs (2 hours) (2 questions)

23. Which of the following would most likely prevent a closing from taking place?
    a. the imposition of discount points by the lender
    b. the hiring of an attorney by the purchaser
    c. the existence of outstanding unpaid liens against the property
    d. a purchase money mortgage given to the seller by the purchaser

24. On the closing statement, which of the following appears as a buyer credit?
    a. earnest money deposit
    b. prepaid real property taxes
    c. prepaid insurance premium
    d. sale of personal property

The Contract of Sale and Leases
Leases (1 hour) (1 question)

25. A lease that automatically renews itself for another time frame at the end of the lease term unless notice is given to terminate is a(n):
    a. illegal lease
    b. periodic lease
    c. standard lease
    d. proprietary lease

The Contract of Sale and Leases
Contracts (1 hour) (1 questions)

26. An option is a contract that:
    a. specifies a time limit within which the optionee may choose to purchase or lease real property
    b. is a bilateral implied contract
    c. does not define a specific sales price
    d. conveys title when the optionee signs the contract

The Contract of Sale and Leases
Contract Preparation (1 hour) (1 question)

27. Which of the following is NOT a part of a real estate contract of sale?
    a. contingency
    b. addenda
    c. rider
    d. codicil

Real Estate Finance (5 hours) (5 questions)

28. A HUD agency that purchases VA and FHA mortgages on the secondary mortgage market is called:
    a. RHA
    b. SONYMA
    c. Ginnie Mae
    d. FDIC

29. A mortgage clause that allows a lender to declare the balance due if the borrower sells the property is the:
    a. prepayment penalty clause
    b. alienation clause
    c. granting clause
    d. defeasance clause

30. A mortgage that provides for paying the debt by monthly payment of principal and interest and in which the interest portion of the payments decreases as the principal portion increases is a(n):
    a. balloon mortgage
    b. installment land contract
    c. swing loan
    d. amortized mortgage

31. The federal law that provides for accurate advertising of financial credit terms is called:
    a. The Real Estate Settlement Procedures Act
    b. Regulation Z
    c. The Community Development Act
    d. Anti-Predatory Lending Law

32. A type of loan in which the mortgage rate floats based on the fluctuations of a standard index is called a(n):
    a. adjustable rate mortgage
    b. straight term mortgage
    c. fixed rate mortgage
    d. fluctuating mortgage

Land Use Regulations (3 hours) (3 questions)

33. Marcia has recently purchased an old barn in a rural community in upstate New York and wishes to turn it into an art studio. Which administrative body must she apply to for a variance? The:
    a. town planning board
    b. zoning board of appeals
    c. local building department
    d. county clerk

34. A document that shows the boundaries and physical dimensions of a property is called a(n):
    a. feasibility study
    b. plat
    c. survey
    d. architectural rending

35. Parks and forest land could be classified as being in which zone?
    a. commercial
    b. residential
    c. public open space
    d. institutional

Construction and Environment (5 hours) (5 questions)

36. A sprayed insulation that caused noxious fumes is called:
    a. loose fill insulation
    b. rigid insulation
    c. UFFI
    d. batt insulation

37. The amount of electrical current flowing through a wire is called:
    a. voltage
    b. amperage
    c. milligaus
    d. wattage

38. The New York statute that mandates minimum R-factors for insulation is the:
    a. Real Property Law
    b. Energy Code
    c. Emergency Tenant Protection Act
    d. Sanitary Code

39. Which of the following is exempt from disclosure regulations of the Residential Lead-Based Hazard Reduction Act?
    a. a duplex built before 1978
    b. a single-family residence built before 1978
    c. senior citizen housing
    d. a cooperative apartment built before 1978

40. One of the most prevalent concerns of underground storage tanks is:
    a. leakage
    b. combustion
    c. explosion
    d. fire

Valuation Process and Pricing Properties (3 hours)(3 questions)

41. One of the most important factors in selecting comparables for a comparative market analysis is to select properties:
    a. within a 50-mile radius of the subject property
    b. older than the subject property
    c. as close in location as possible to the comparable
    d. that have inferior curb appeal to the subject property

42. Surveyors' and appraisers' fees in relation to the development of a property are called:
    a. hard costs
    b. indirect costs
    c. direct costs
    d. impact fees

43. An arm's length transaction means that:
    a. the parties are not related either as relatives or business associates
    b. no salesperson or broker is involved in the transaction
    c. the transaction is a cash transaction and no financing is required
    d. the transaction takes place within six months of being placed on the market

Human Rights and Fair Housing (4 hours) (4 questions)

44. Hattie wants to sell her home in Kingston, New York. She decides not to use a broker so that she can sell her property to whomever she wants. Which of the following is TRUE? Hattie:
    a. is exempt from all fair housing laws as long as she does not use a broker
    b. is exempt from fair housing laws in the sale of a single-family home
    c. can only sell her property to whomever she want if she does not advertise
    d. and/or a broker are not entitled to any exemptions to fair housing laws in the sale of a single-family home in New York

45. The fine for a first offense in violation of the Federal Fair Housing Act can be up to:
    a. $1,000
    b. $5,000
    c. $10,000
    d. $20,000

46. Which of the following is required by law for real estate brokers?
    a. memorizing the NYS Division of Human Rights poster
    b. prominently displaying the HUD fair housing poster
    c. accepting all real estate listings
    d. keeping a copy of the New York Human Rights Law in the office as a reference

47. One of the differences between federal human rights law and New York human rights law is that the:
    a. federal law does not address discrimination based on familial status and the New York law does
    b. federal law does not address discrimination based on disability and the New York law does
    c. federal law has fewer protected classes than the New York law
    d. federal law does not address discrimination based on sex and the New York law does

Real Estate Mathematics (1 hour) (2 questions)

48. If Calvin buys three parcels of land for $8,000 and sells them as four separate parcels for $9,000 each, what percent profit does he make?
    a. 33%
    b. 40 %
    c. 45%
    d. 50%

49. The owner of a rectangular parcel of land measuring 500 feet wide (front) by 150 feet long is offered $20 per front foot or $5,000 per acre. What is the amount of the higher offer?
    a. $3,469
    b. $6,400
    c. $10,000
    d. $12,500

Municipal Agencies (2 hours) (2 questions)

50. Which of the following is NOT a function of the building department?
    a. code compliance
    b, requiring landowners to restore or rehabilitate a historic structure
    c. inspection during construction
    d. issuing building permits

51. Evie wants to grant an area of undeveloped wetlands to her town. What agency would most likely accept this grant?
    a. conservation advisory council
    b. planning board
    c. architectural review board
    d. building department

Property Insurance (2 hours) (2 questions)

52. Which of the following is FALSE?
    a. lenders require homeowner's insurance to obtain a mortgage
    b. perils are events that are always excluded from payment on the insurance policy
    c. an endorsement is an attachment to the insurance policy
    d. an insurance policy is a legal contract

53. Sam has an HO-3 homeowner's policy. When his storage shed was damaged in a fire, he received $20,000 on his insurance claim. Based on this information, what amount of insurance did he have on the residence?
    a. $100,000
    b. $120,000
    c. $150,000
    d. $200,000

Taxes and Assessments (3 hours) (3 questions)

54. If the assessor determines that the market value of a property is $300,000, and the level of assessment (LOA) in the taxing unit is 75 percent, what is the assessment for that property?
    a. $200,000
    b. $225,000
    c. $250,000
    d. $275,000

55. Property owners are charged an extra amount on their property tax bill for the addition of three new fire trucks in the taxing unit. This charge is known as a (n):
    a. tax certiorari
    b. reassessment
    c. special assessment
    d. tax levy

56. A legal action brought by the taxing authority when real property taxes are not paid when due is a (n):
    a. in rem legal proceeding
    b. injunction
    c. Article 78 proceeding
    d. reformation

Condominiums and Cooperatives (4 hours) (3 questions)

57. In a cooperative, who is generally in charge of the approval of the prospective buyer of a cooperative unit? The:
    a. lender
    b. board of directors
    c. vote of the majority of the share holders
    d. the management company

58. In a cooperative, who owns the common areas? The:
    a. the management company
    b. the unit owner
    c. cooperative corporation
    d. all of the above

59. The terms under which a cooperative gives permission to a shareholder to make any structural changes to the individual unit is called:
    a. a letter of intent
    b. house rules
    c. a subscription agreement
    d. an alteration agreement

Commercial and Investment Properties (10 hours) (9 questions)

60. An investor purchases a $2,300,000 apartment complex with a $600,000 down payment. Each month the cash flow from rentals, less expenses, is $20,000. Over a year's time, the cash-on-cash return would be:
    a. 25 percent
    b. 28 percent
    c. 32 percent
    d. 40 percent

61. The profit from income producing property, less income taxes, is known as:
    a. after tax cash flow
    b. before tax cash flow
    c. debt service
    d. the debt-to- equity ratio

62. If a property generates a $10,000 cash flow and a $2,000 tax loss that is used to offset other income, the after-tax cash flow for an investor in the 35 percent tax bracket is:
    a. $3,560
    b. $4,200
    c. $4,320
    d. $5,490

63. A paper income loss on investment property that is sometimes desirable to property owners is known as:
    a. gross income
    b. debt service
    c. leverage
    d. a tax shelter

64. What is the value estimate of a property (rounded) if the net operating income is $650,000 and the capitalization rate is 12 percent?
    a. $678,000
    b. $4,678,000
    c. $5,216,000
    d. $5,416,667

65. Generally, property owners lease commercial space according to the:
    a. rentable square footage
    b. usable square footage
    c. effective square footage
    d. carpetable area

66. Commercial lessees may view the difference between the rentable and usable area in a commercial space as which of the following?
    a. vacancy factor
    b. loss factor
    c. unused perimeter
    d. common areas

67. One of the main differences between a loft and other types of commercial space for a lease is that a loft:
    a. is not usually divided into rooms
    b. is always more expensive per square foot than other types of space
    c. always has a private elevator
    d. is generally under rent control

68. A lease agreement for commercial property is generally:
    a. standard throughout the state
    b. customized to the particular space and tenant
    c. for ten years or more
    d. a periodic lease

Income Tax Issues in Real Estate Transactions (3 hours) (3 questions)

69. JayCee paid $400,000 for an investment property. She also has a loss of $50,000 due to a fire. She values her property at $350,000. This value is which of the following?
    a. appraised value
    b. adjusted basis
    c. basis
    d. market value

70. Harry has an ownership interest in a 60-unit apartment building as a limited partner. According to IRS rules, this kind of ownership is:
    a. active income
    b. passive income
    c. portfolio income
    d. deductible income

71. In a tax-deferred exchange, the individual who accepts the funds from the sale and handles the contracts is called the:
    a. arbitrator
    b. mediator
    c. qualified intermediary
    d. coordinator

Mortgage Brokerage (1 hour) (2 questions)

72. Which of the following documents do mortgage brokers use to make certain disclosures to potential borrowers?
    a. agency disclosure form
    b. pre-approval letter
    c. letter of intent
    d. pre-application disclosure and fee agreement

73. Which of the following is FALSE? A (n) mortgage banker:
    a. may lend money
    b. may collect the loan payments
    c. closes the loan in its own name
    d. is licensed by the Federal Deposit Insurance Corporation

Property Management (2 hours) (2 questions)

74. The property manager's fee is generally which of the following?
    a. a percentage of all rental income when the rent roll exceeds a certain pre agreed upon amount
    b. a lump sum paid in advance on a yearly basis
    c. 25 percent of the rental income
    d. a base fee and a percentage of the rents collected

75. Laurel, a real estate broker, is also a property manager for an eight-unit residential property. In her role as property manager, Laurel is a (n):
    a. general agent
    b. fiduciary
    c. special agent
    d. both a and b

Answer Key

All answers provided are referenced to the *New York Real Estate for Salespersons, 4th e,* by Marcia Darvin Spada, Cengage Learning 2009.

Answer Key for Review Questions

License Law and Regulations

1. D
A licensee must only accept a commission from his sponsoring broker so this is not a violation of the license law.
REF: p. 23

2. D
Building superintendents working for one owner, public officers, and attorneys who do not employ salesperson do not require a license. Auctioneers who sell real property must have a real estate license.
REF: p. 13

3. B
A licensee who deposits an earnest money check in his personal checking account instead of in the broker's trust account is guilty of commingling. Conversion is the illegal use of another's money. Escheat is the state's right to a decedent's property if no heirs are found.
REF: p. 27

4. C
A major purpose of the license law is to protect the public.
REF: p. 10

5. C
A broker must complete 120 hours of qualifying education.
REF: p. 11

6. B
The regulatory agency that oversees the licensure process in New York is the Department of State.
REF: p. 10

7. B
The minimum age for salesperson licensure is 18.
REF: p. 11

8. C
Individuals do not need U.S. citizenship to obtain a salesperson license in New York.
REF: p. 11

9. C

When transacting real estate business, a licensee must carry his pocket card.
REF: p. 18

10. A

Licensees must complete continuing education requirements every two years upon license renewal unless exempt.
REF: p. 20

Law of Agency
Part I Agency
11. B

A broker's commission is determined by agreement between the broker and principal. There are no set fee schedules for broker commissions.
REF: p. 47

12. D

In the sale of one- to four-unit residential real estate, a listing agent must first disclose her status to a prospective buyer at the first substantive meeting such as when the listing contract is signed.
REF: p. 73

13. B

A person empowered to act on behalf of another is called the agent. The principal is the party the agent represents. A party of the first part is the grantor on a deed.
REF: p. 41

14. C

In this example, Danielle must have signed an exclusive right-to-sell agreement that states that she must pay Robert his commission no matter who sells the property.
REF: p. 65

15. A

A buyer broker who represents the buyer as a client can never be a subagent of the seller which implies seller representation.
REF: p. 62

16. D

An agency relationship is always consensual. There has to be an agreement between the parties.
REF: p. 41

17. A

The most common agency relationship that brokers have with their principals is as a special agent. A general agent manages various affairs pertaining to the property. A power of attorney is permission to handle the limited affairs of another. A universal agency is an all-encompassing power of attorney.
REF: 44

18. D

If there is no specific contact with an agent and no substantive contact, then the agency disclosure form is not required.
REF: p. 71

19. B

Price fixing occurs when competitors in a certain group charge the same or similar price. A group boycott is a conspiracy in which a person or group is coerced into not doing business with another person or group. An illegal market allocation agreement occurs when competing companies agree to split a territory among them. A tie-in arrangement occurs when a party selling a service to a buyer, as a condition of sale, has the buyer purchase another product from the seller.
REF: p. 49

20. D

A tie-in arrangement occurs when a party selling a service to a buyer, as a condition of sale, has the buyer purchase another product from the seller. A group boycott is a conspiracy in which a person or group is coerced into not doing business with another person or group. Price fixing occurs when competitors in a certain group charge the same or similar price. An illegal market allocation agreement occurs when competing companies agree to split a territory among them.
REF: p. 50

Law of Agency
Part II Independent Contractor
21. A

In general, most real estate licensees, through an agreement with the broker, and allowable under IRS law, are independent contractors.
REF: p. 78

22. D

An associate broker-independent contractor can be an office manager.
REF: p. 18

23. D

There is no law that says a broker must accompany a sales agent/independent contract when showing a property. However, the seller may request this.
REF: p. 81

24. A

IRS regulations require that the sales agent enter into an independent contractor agreement with the broker.
REF: p. 79

25. B

In order to qualify under IRS regulations for independent contractor status, the sales agent must be licensed.
REF: p.78

26. C

The IRS requires the filing of Form 1099 misc. for all independent contractors who earn $600 in the calendar tax year.
REF: p. 79

27. D

Independent contractors must file yearly federal and state tax returns just as employees do.
REF: p. 79

28. C

In New York, brokers must keep records as to the sale or mortgage of one-to-four unit properties for at least three years.
REF: p. 80

29. B

Under IRS regulations, although a salesperson is an independent contractor, the broker supervises the sales agent.
REF: p. 78

30. D

The salesperson-independent contractor is responsible for all withholding and other tax obligations.
REF: pp.78-79

Legal Issues
Part I Estates and Interests
31. D

The term, pur autre vie, means *for another life*, therefore, the terms refers to a life estate measured by the life of someone other than the life tenant.
REF: p. 102

32. C

Real property is in a fixed place.
REF: p. 95

33. B

Tenants by the entirety refer to husband and wife.
REF: p. 106

34. D

Public parks and historical monuments are examples of special purpose real estate.
REF: p. 98

35. A

A life estate is ownership or possession for someone's lifetime. A leasehold estate is a rental estate with possession, not ownership.
REF: p. 101

36. B

Fee simple absolute, fee simple defeasible, and fee simple on condition all imply some form of ownership. A leasehold estate implies possession, not ownership.
REF: p. 100

37. A

Because the condition states that the daughter cannot use the property for commercial purposes, the example is a fee simple on condition.
REF: p. 101

38. A

Ownership in severalty refers to ownership by one owner. Think of it as the owner is "severed" from others.

REF: p. 103

39. B

Chattel is another term for personal property.

REF: p. 96

40. A

An estate for years can be for any fixed time as short as one day. Joint tenancy is a type of ownership. Usury is a practice that charges more interest than is lawfully allowed.

REF: p. 169

Legal Issues
Part II Liens and Easements

41. C

A lien is a claim that one person has against the property of another for a debt.

REF: p. 110

42. B

An easement is a nonpossessory use of land by another.

REF: p. 114

43. A

The meaning of the term, lis pendens, is that a lawsuit is pending.

REF: p. 111

44. C

Mortgages are voluntary because a mortgagor wants the mortgage and creates a specific lien against the real property.

REF: p. 110

45. D

A mechanic's lien is involuntary because it is against the lienee and creates a specific lien against the real property.

REF: p. 113

46. B

Although certain types of liens have priority over other types, the factor that determines the priority is the time and date of filing.

REF: p. 113

47. A

Utility companies obtain an easement in gross. Easement appurtenant describes all other types of easements. Easement by prescription and easement by grant are specific ways in which easements are created.

REF: p. 114

48. C

The dominant tenement is the property that benefits from the easements. The servient tenement is the property that allows the easement and where the easement is located.

REF: p. 115

49. D

Items that extend into another's property are called encroachments. Easements are nonpossessory interests in another's property.
Ref: p. 117

50. C

A license is a temporary privilege.
REF: p. 119

Legal Issues
Part III Deeds

51. C

The deed is the document that conveys title to real property.
REF: p. 119

52. C

In Latin, habendum means to have, so the clause means "to have to and to hold."
The defeasance clause appears in a mortgage.
REF: p. 120

53. D

A quitclaim deed has the least guarantee of title. A full covenant and warranty deed has the broadest guarantee of title. A deed of trust is a financing instrument.
REF: p. 126

54. C

To execute a deed or any other legal document means to sign it.
REF: p. 120

55. B

The party that conveys title to real property is the grantor. The grantee receives title and is the party of the second part on the deed.
REF: p.119

56. A

The legal term for the transfer of property is called alienation. Lis pendens is type of notice indicating that a legal action is pending.
REF: p. 119

57. B

A correction deed may be ordered by the court to correct a typographical error. All of the other deeds in the question are judicial deeds.
REF: p.129

58. C

A type of property description used in a deed that starts with a point or place of beginning is called a metes and bounds description. Description by monument may refer to a large rock or other landmark and is not commonly used in New York. Description by lot and block, sometimes found on a deed, refers to the location of the property. Description by reference links the description to another document such as a plat or tax map.
REF: p. 123

59. A

When a landowner donates a parcel of land for public use, this is called dedication. Adverse possession is a method of acquiring title to real property by conforming to certain statutory requirements.
REF: p. 130

60. D

The person appointed in a will to carry out its provisions is the executor. The legatee receives something from the will. A testator or devisor is one who makes a will. A woman is a testatrix.
REF: p. 130

Legal Issues
Part IV Title Closing and Costs

61. C

Title to real estate is transferred upon execution and delivery of a valid deed.
REF: p. 119

62. A

Generally, in the closing process, attorneys for a lender represent the best interests of the lending institution. The purchasers' attorney, if they hire one, represents their best interests.
REF: p. 132-133

63. D

A federal statute that regulates disclosure and closing requirements for mortgage loans on residential property is the Real Estate Settlement Procedures Act. The Truth-in-Lending Act promotes the informed use of consumer credit. The Interstate Land Sales is a federal law regulating the sale across state lines of subdivided land.
REF: p. 140

64. C

The successive conveyances of title, starting with the current deed and going back an appropriate time (typically 40 to 60 years) is the chain of title; title must be unbroken to be good and, therefore, marketable.
REF: p. 135

65. B

The document that illustrates the measurement, boundaries, and area of a property is called a survey. A feasibility study determines a project's usefulness and projected success in the community. A plat is subdivision map.
REF: p. 133

66. A

A condensed history pertaining to the title of a property is called an abstract of title. A chain of title is the successive conveyances of title to a property. Title insurance insures the policy owner against loss if the title is not good.
REF: p. 135

67. D

One of the most important roles of a licensee just before closing is to arrange and accompany a prospective purchaser through a final inspection of the property. Generally, attorneys examine the deed, prepare the abstract of title, and prepare the closing statement.
REF: p. 137

68. B

A New York tax on the conveyance of title to real property is called the real estate transfer tax. The capital gains tax is a federal tax on profits from the sale of real estate. The mortgage recording fee is the charge for recording a mortgage.
REF: p. 141

69. A

Unpaid utility bills are the responsibility of the seller at closing.
REF: p. 146

70. C

The seller will not require mortgage insurance as his mortgage will generally be paid off at closing.
REF: p. 146

The Contract of Sale and Leases
Part I Leases
71. A

A periodic lease automatically renews itself at the end of the term unless notice is given.
REF: p. 169

72. B

A leasehold estate implies possession, not ownership. Therefore, it is never conveyed by a deed.
REF: p. 168

73. C

An estate at will can be for any timeframe. A periodic estate automatically renews itself unless notice is given. A freehold estate is an ownership estate.
REF: p. 169

74. B

A tenant who was originally in lawful possession of the premises but does not leave after the right to possession ends is a holdover tenant. A trespasser was never in lawful possession in the first place.
REF: 169

75. C

A lease is a type of contract. A deed is not contract but an option and a promissory note are.
REF: p. 168

76. D

There are no statutory requirements for the term of a lease in New York. It can be for one-day and for any specified duration.
REF: p. 170

77. D
According to New York law, leases must be in clear language and appropriately captioned.
REF: p. 174

78. C
Should there be an emergency; the landlord has a right to enter a premises without specific permission in the lease.
REF: p. 176

79. A
If a tenant is forced to leave the premises because of lack of basic services, it may be a constructive eviction. Actual eviction occurs when a landlord physically forces tenants to leave the premises. A lis pendens is a pending lawsuit regarding a property
REF: p. 178

80. D
A new owner of a leased property must abide by all of the terms of the leases that are in place at the time and may not make changes until lease expiration.
REF: p. 179

The Contract of Sale and Leases
Part II Contracts
81. B
Consideration is the giving of something of value as an inducement to contract. Quiet enjoyment has to do with possession of one's property. A power of attorney gives a person authority to act for another in legal matters.
REF: p.184

82. C
Many real estate contracts do not require financing so financing is not an essential element of a valid contract.
REF: p. 184

83. C
The rule that requires real estate contracts are in writing is called the Statute of Frauds.
The Statute of Limitations addresses time limits to sue. The Real Estate Settlement Procedures Act addresses lender disclosures for closings. The Uniform Commercial Code regulates commercial paper (notes, drafts, checks.)
REF: pp. 184-185

84. B
A contract between two parties who have definitely agreed to the contract terms is called an express bilateral contract.
REF: p. 181-182

85. A
Under an installment land contract, the purchaser does not have legal title to the property. Legal title is conveyed when the contract terms have been fulfilled.
REF: p. 197

86. B
Assignment is the giving over of the contract to another. The contract does not transfer to another with a sublet. Rescission means to annul the contract.
REF: p. 185

87. D
The listing contract between the seller and agent is executory because a buyer has not been found and the contract is not complete. An implied contract arises through the actions of the parties. Void and unenforceable contracts are not valid.
REF:p. 183

88. C
A contract stating, "time is of the essence," means that the contract must be performed on or before the date stipulated in the contract.
REF: p.194

89. B
An earnest money deposit is not legally necessary for an offer to purchase.
REF: p. 187

90. D
A contract with a minor can generally go forward but is voidable by the minor.
REF: p. 184

The Contract of Sale and Leases
Part III Contract Preparation
91. D
Assumable, home equity, and FHA are types of mortgages. A purchase money mortgage is a type of seller financing.
REF: p. 238

92. B
A portion of a property purchase price that is paid in cash and not a part of the mortgage is the down payment. A binder is a type of agreement to purchase. An assumable mortgage is a type of mortgage. A mortgage commitment is a lender's promise to loan a certain amount of funds.
REF: p. 202

93. A
The purchaser is generally the first to sign the contract of sale because he is making the contract offer to the seller.
REF: p. 204

94. D
Raphael's advice regarding the "as is" clause in the contract constitutes the illegal practice of law.
REF: pp. 206-207

95. B
An IOLA account (Interest on Lawyer's Account) is held by an attorney.
REF: p. 203

96. A
The Lawyer Fund for Client Protection has to do with the protection of escrow accounts that attorneys hold for client monies.
REF: p. 203

97. C
The accepted practice in many upstate areas is for the broker to hold a purchaser's deposit in escrow until closing. Should a salesperson receive a deposit check, he must turn it over to his broker.
REF: p. 203

98. C
A customary deposit is 10 percent of the purchase price, so Keri would put down a deposit of $45,000. This percentage can vary from deal to deal.
REF: p. 203

99. C
A contract of sale is binding when the attorney for each party approves the contract.
REF: p. 206

100. D
A survey, certificate of occupancy, and prior deed are all used by attorneys and others to prepare for a closing. A census statement is not necessary.
REF: p. 200

Real Estate Finance
101. C
The mortgagor is the borrower. The mortgagee is the lender.
REF: p. 228

102. A
The mortgagee is the lender. The mortgagor is the borrower.
REF: p. 228

103. B
A mortgage is a written document pledging a property as security for the repayment of a loan.
REF: p. 228

104. D
VA loans up to a certain amount do not require a down payment.
REF: p. 243

105. B
A balloon mortgage is best described as having a larger payment due at the end of its term.
REF: p. 255

106. A
When a lender is willing to lower the interest rate at the time the loan is made in return for extra payments of points up front, this is called a buydown. Usury is the charging of a higher interest rate than allowed by law. A satisfaction of mortgage is a document stating that the mortgage debt is fully paid.
REF: p. 234

107. D

An amortized mortgage loan is one that is paid in monthly payments of both principal and interest
REF: p. 236

108. C

A wraparound mortgage is a subordinate mortgage that includes the same principal obligation secured by a first mortgage against the same property. It is a type of seller financing.
REF: p. 238

109. B

A satisfaction of mortgage is a document from the lender stating that the loan is paid in full. A certificate of tile sets forth the title examiner's opinion of the title. HUD Form No. 1 is used by lenders to itemize closing costs.
REF: p. 235

110. B

The New York agency that raises money from tax free bonds and applies
the money to mortgage loans is called SONYMA. Fannie Mae (short for Federal National Mortgage Association) is part of the secondary mortgage market. FDIC is a federal agency that protects bank deposits. RHA (the Rural Housing Authority) is a federal agency that makes loans for rural housing.
REF: 244

Land Use Regulations
111. D

Eminent domain allows government to take property for public use only if it is for the use and benefit of the public. Escheat allows property to revert to the state only if heirs cannot be found. Zoning ordinances are public land use controls and deed restrictions are private land use controls.
REF: p. 266

112. A

The doctrine of laches refers to a loss of legal rights because of failure to assert them.
REF: p. 263

113. B

The New York law that protects residents in the purchase of vacant subdivided land sold on the installment plan is Article 9-A of the Real Property Law. Article 12-A is a New York law pertaining to salespersons and brokers. The Statute of Frauds states that contracts that create an interest in real estate must be in writing.
REF: 265

114. C

When property reverts to the state due to the lack of heirs, it is called escheat. Eminent domain is the governments right to take property for the use and benefit of the public with just compensation.
REF: p. 268

115. C

The agency that coordinates information relevant to an environmental impact statement is called the lead agency. The zoning board of appeals oversees variance requests.
REF: p. 264

116. A
Zoning ordinances are an example of a government's police power.
REF: pp. 264-265

117. D
Local building departments oversee building code compliance. The zoning board of appeals oversees variance requests. HUD is a federal agency that oversees housing issues. The Department of Environmental Conservation oversees water-related issues.
REF: p. 266

118. B
An in-law apartment that is connected to a residential home is called an accessory use.
REF: p. 269

119. A
Hospitals, schools, and courthouses are examples of institutional zoning. Public open space includes parks.
REF: p. 270

120. B
The imposition of a delay in developing property in a given area is a moratorium. Transfer of development rights involve the exchange of zoning privileges from areas with low population needs, such as farmland, to areas of high population needs, such as downtown areas. Demographics is the study of the social and economic statistics of a community. Infrastructure refers to the support systems of a community
REF: p. 274

Construction and Environmental Issues
Part I Construction
121. D
The NYS Department of Health furnishes guidelines for minimum separation distances between a well and a septic system and other sanitary guidelines.
REF: p. 287

122. C
Insulation has to do with the interior of the structure, not the exterior or site.
REF: p. 299

123. B
The concrete base below the frost line that supports the foundation of a
structure is the footing. The foundation rests upon the footing. A slab on grade is a type of foundation. A girder is a support beam.
REF: p. 291

124. A
The wooden skeleton of a residential structure of a residential property is called the frame. It is composed of wooden framing members.
REF: p. 293

125. C
Openings for doors and windows in a residential property are supported by headers. Lally columns are support columns. Rafters are framing members for the roof. The sill plate is the base for the framing.
REF: p. 295

126. B
The R- factor is a measure of heat transfer through the walls of a structure. The greater the degree of insulation, the greater the R-factor.
REF: p. 298

127. D
A type of heating system that heats water in a boiler and then uses circulator pumps to propel the heated water to convectors is called a hot water system. Forced warm air systems include a duct system that blows warm air. A heat pump produces cool and warm air.
REF: p. 300

128. A
The water supply and waste water systems are always separated with two different piping systems. The supply pipes bring clean water into the structure and the waste water systems carries used water from the structure.
REF: p. 302

129. B
The minimum electrical service installed in a residential home must be 100 amps but is often higher.
REF: p. 304

130. A
A device that melts and open a circuit to stop electrical power when overheating occurs is called a fuse. The distribution panel is where the fuses or circuit breakers are located. The service drop is the electrical service coming into the property.
REF: p. 305

Construction and Environmental Issues
Part II Environmental Issues
131. D
The Superfund Amendments and Reauthorization Act imposed stringent cleanup standards and expanded the definition of those responsible for clean up. The National Environmental Policy Act and Clean Air Act are other federal environmental laws. The State Environmental Quality Review is a New York law.
REF: p. 323

132. B
Drinking water safety is overseen by the NYS Department of Health.
REF: p. 310

133. C
One of the biggest dangers in highly corrosive water is that it may contain large amounts of lead. Although radon may enter a house through water, i.e., the shower, it is a gas and not corrosive. PCBs are a byproduct of electrical transformers. CFCs do not appear in water.
REF: p. 311

134. A
The NYS Department of Environmental Conservation licenses pest inspectors in New York.
REF: p. 312

135. B
Asbestos is a fibrous mineral that was used in many construction applications in the past but is no longer used.
REF: p. 314

136. D
The Residential Leadbased Hazard Reduction Act calls for a mutually agreeable 10-day period for a lead paint assessment before a purchaser becomes obligated under a contract. The Act applies to target properties built before 1978.
REF: p. 315

137. D
Radon most generally enters the home through small cracks in the foundation wall. This is because radon comes from the ground.
REF: p. 319

138. A
No level of radon is considered safe. If a property has more than 4 picocuries of radon, remediation is generally necessary.
REF: p. 320

139. B
If the indoor air quality of a commercial building causes large numbers of people to fall ill, the building is said to have sick building syndrome.
REF: p. 322-323

140. D
A toxic liquid organic compound used as an insulating medium for electrical transformers and has polluted the soil and waterways is called PCBs. Radon is a radioactive gas. UFFI is an insulation that contains formaldehyde. Chlorofluorocarbons are a chemical that is dangerous to our ozone layer.
REF: p. 323

Valuation Process and Pricing Properties
141. C
An analysis of the competition in the market place that a property will face upon sale attempts is called a comparative market analysis. An appraisal employs at least one of the approaches to value such as the cost approach. An evaluation may not be used to find a value of the project.
REF: p. 343

142. D
The income, sales, and cost approach are all appraisal approaches to value. The comparative market analysis is not.
REF: p 348

143. C

An owner who uses a residential house for vacation purposes only may attribute value in use to this property. Assessed value is applied by an assessor, insurance value is replacement value, and investment value is the return expected by an investor.
REF: p. 340

144. A

Feasibility studies, highest and best use studies, and land utilization studies are all forms of evaluation studies. An appraisal of a single-family home is an estimate of value.
REF: p. 340

145. D

A property will probably NOT sell for market value if it is an arm's length transaction since the buyer and seller may know one another.
REF: p.342

146. D

Price is not always equivalent to the market value of the property. It may be either more or less.
REF: p. 342

147. C

If there are construction problems and time constraints, the cost of the property may be below market value. One reason is that time is money.
REF: p. 342

148. D

Indirect costs are the costs of architectural, engineering, licensing, permits and other expenses. Hard or direct costs are for labor and materials.
REF: p. 342

149. A

Comparables used in the creation of a comparative market analysis should be as similar as possible to the subject property.
REF: p. 352

150. C

Properties yet to be built are not an appropriate comparable for a comparative market analysis because market conditions may be different when these properties are placed on the market.
REF: p. 352

Human Rights and Fair Housing

151. C

Redlining is an illegal practice by lenders that excludes people from culturally diverse neighborhoods from receiving housing loans. Steering is a violation of the Federal Fair Housing Act and is practice by real estate brokers that encourages culturally diverse people toward or away from certain areas.
REF:p. 375

152. A

The Civil Rights Act of 1866 prohibits all discrimination based on race in the buying, selling, and leasing of property-no exceptions.
REF: p. 367

153. B

Under the Federal Fair Housing Act, an administrative law judge may impose up to a 50,000 fine for a "pattern of discrimination."

REF: p. 369

154. D

Blockbusting occurs when real estate salespeople tell homeowners that a member of a protected class is moving into their neighborhood causing them to panic and place their homes for sale.

REF: p. 374

155. A

Steering occurs when real estate agents lead prospective homeowners toward or away from certain areas.

REF: p. 362

156. C

One of the differences between the federal Fair Housing Law and the New York Human Rights Law is that the New York law covers commercial property as well as residential. There are other differences such as New York has more protected classes that the federal law does.

REF: p. 370-371

157. D

The Americans with Disabilities Act covers buildings open to the public as well as multifamily dwellings.

REF: p. 370

158. B

In addition to federal law, protected classes under the New York Human Rights Law include age and marital status. Other protected classes in New York, not covered by federal law, include sexual orientation and military status.

REF: p. 371

159. B

Nancy cannot discriminate because of race in the rental of her apartment. The Civil Rights Act of 1866 prohibits all racial discrimination. There are no exemptions.

REF: p. 371

160. A

An area designated by the Department of State where salesperson and brokers may not solicit listings is in a cease and desist zone. Homeowners may request that the DOS place them on a cease and desist list.

REF: p. 373

Real Estate Mathematics

161. B

$12,500 ÷ 0.07 = $178, 571

REF: p. 389

162. D

$8,250 ÷ 0.075 = $110,000

REF: p. 389

163. C
$475,000 x .0.02 = $9,500
$475,000 + $9,500 = $484,500
$484,500 x 0.02 = $9,690
$484,500 + $9,690 = $494,190
REF: p. 391

164. A
52 x 162 = 8,424 square feet
$75,000 ÷ 8,424 = $8.90
REF: p. 392

165. C
43,560 ÷ 425 = 102.5 feet (rounded)
REF: p. 392

166. D
$175,000 x 0.90 = $157,500
REF: p. 398

167. B
$2,500 ÷ 12 = $208.33
$208.33 ÷ 2 = $104.17
$208.33 + $104.17 = $312.50
REF: p. 151

168. C
$120,000 x 0.80 = $96,000
$96,000 x 0.03 = $2,880
REF: p. 382

169. A
$50,000 x 0.095 = $4,750
REF: p. 397

170. B
$2,304 ÷ 0.024 = $96,000
$96,000 ÷0.80 = $120,000
REF: pp. 399-400

Municipal Agencies
171. B
The legislative power of a city is vested in its city council. The legislative power of towns is vested in the town council; and in villages, in the village board of trustees.
REF: p. 405

172. D
The main function of a city or town planning board is to advise on land use matters.
REF: p. 407

173. C

In most cities and towns, the zoning boards of appeals or other similar agencies hear variance requests. The town board deals with policy and laws and the planning board deals with land use issues

REF: p. 408

174. A

In many municipalities, the conservation advisory council advises on wetland regulations. The architectural review board oversees building design. The zoning board of appeals hears various requests.

REF: p. 409

175. D

Building departments do not rule on variance applications. This is performed by another agency, usually the zoning board of appeals.

REF: p. 411

176. C

The document containing each property's assessment in a municipality is the assessment roll. The tax map shows the boundaries and measurements of lots in the taxing jurisdiction.

REF: p. 412

177. B

In some cities and towns, the official or agency that collects fees for water usage and other permits is the receiver of taxes. The tax assessor performs assessments.

REF: p. 412

178. A

The New York state agency that oversees wetland regulations is the Department of Environmental Conservation. The Department of Health oversees water related issues, disease control, and licensing of physicians, and other health professionals.

REF: p. 409

179. B

A town or village planning board consists of five to seven members who are appointed.

REF: p. 407

180. D

The historic preservation commission, zoning board of appeals, and building department would most likely deal with renovating historic property. The conservation advisory council usually deals with environmental issues.

REF: p. 409

Property Insurance

181. A

A clause in an insurance policy that changes or modifies the policy is called an endorsement. A peril is a kind of known hazard. A deductible is the amount the insured must pay towards a claim before receiving any policy benefits. An umbrella policy is an excess liability policy, providing additional coverage above that offered by primary policies.

REF: 425

182. B

Insurance obtained through the New York Property Insurance Underwriting Association can be undesirable because the premiums are higher than those obtained through the voluntary market.
REF: p. 426

183. B

FEMA (Federal Emergency Management Agency) administers the National Flood Insurance Program. Local programs work with FEMA.
REF: p. 427

184. D

In New York, a windstorm deductible must be disclosed to the insured.
REF: p. 428

185. C

As long as the insurance company states the reason for the cancellation, an insurance policy may be cancelled within 60 days. Other insurance department regulations apply to cancellations.
REF: p. 428

186. D

The cost of a homeowner's policy is directly related to both the policyholder and the property. There are no statewide fee schedules.
REF: p. 428

187. C

The insured must pay a deductible before receiving policy benefits from a claim. A premium is the amount of money the property owner must pay for insurance coverage. Perils are events that do damage. An endorsement is a document attached to the policy that modifies or changes the original policy in some way.
REF: p. 428

188. B

An umbrella policy is an excess liability policy, providing additional coverage above that offered by primary policies. A homeowner's special form policy is a type of homeowners insurance.
REF: p. 429

189. A

The declarations page of the policy outlines the basic coverage contained in the policy.
REF: p. 422

190. D

Functional obsolescence is flawed or faulty property rendered inferior because of advances and change. This is not specifically covered in the insurance policy.
REF: p. 349

191. C

Government buildings such as a VA hospital and state office building are property tax exempt as well as religious organizations such as a synagogue. Gas stations are private and not tax exempt.
REF: p.436

192. C

The tax rate is determined by the amount of the tax levy. The assessor values property for tax purposes.
REF: p.438

193. B

The percentage at which properties are assessed in a locality is called the level of assessment. The tax levy is the amount that a municipality must raise to meet budgetary requirements. The residential assessment ratio (RAR) is the assessed value divided by the sales price of the property. The tax rate is the amount of money needed by a municipality to meet budgetary requirements divided by the taxable assessed and nonexempt value of all the real property within that jurisdiction.
REF: p. 438

194. D

Reassessments can be performed on properties when improvements are made, and on a regular prescribed basis.
REF: p. 441

195. D

Cities, towns, and villages may be taxing jurisdictions. The state does not collect property taxes.
REF: p. 436

196. B

People with disabilities, seniors, and veterans can be partially exempt from paying real property taxes. Property owners under 25 are not if the only reason is their age.
REF: pp. 444-445

197. D

The purpose of the board of assessment review is to hear grievances. Taxes are levied by the taxing jurisdiction, and uniform percentages are determined by the taxing jurisdiction. The equalization rate is developed by the NYS Office of Real Property Services.
REF: p. 446

198. B

If a property owner believes that his property's assessed value is greater than the property's full value, he may claim that he has been subject to excessive assessment. Unequal assessment occurs when a property is assessed at a higher percentage of value than the average of all other properties on the same assessment roll. Unlawful assessment includes properties that under law are fully exempt from real property taxation. Misclassification occurs when a property is wrongfully classified on the assessment roll such as if a property is classified as a homestead property when it is a nonhomestead property.
REF: p. 450

199. A

A judicial review of a tax protest in the New York Supreme Court is called a tax certiorari proceeding. A grievance is a property tax complaint brought before the board of assessment review. An Article 78 proceeding is a lawsuit brought against an administrative agency.
REF: p. 451

200. C

The first task in determining the assessment for tax purposes is to establish the market value of each parcel of land within the taxing unit.
REF: pp. 438-439

Condominiums and Cooperatives

201. A

Ownership in a cooperative is evidenced by shares of stock, not a deed. A recognition agreement is an agreement between the cooperative and other entities. An alteration agreement is an agreement for improvements to the unit between the cooperative corporation and the unit owner.
REF: p. 460

202. B

A cooperative owner has a leasehold interest in the unit that is evidenced by a proprietary lease. Freehold and fee simple absolute indicate ownership.
REF: p. 462

203. D

The proprietary lease is given to a cooperative shareholder upon purchase of the unit.
The declaration, prospectus, and initial price of the units are included in the condominium offering plan.
REF: p. 463

204. B

House rules govern daily behavior in the cooperative. The alteration agreement is an agreement between a shareholder and the cooperative corporation to make improvements to the unit. A recognition agreement is an agreement between the cooperative and other entities. A letter of intent is agreement to purchase a condominium that may or may not be binding
REF: pp. 463-464

205. C

Although a board package addresses a number of issues, some of them personal, it mainly consists of financial data.
REF: p. 465

206. D

An agreement that outlines the responsibilities between the cooperative corporation and the lender is called a recognition agreement. The CPS1 statement defines how a condominium or cooperative must be advertised and rules for testing the market before the offering plan is approved by the Attorney General. The alteration agreement is an agreement between a cooperative owner and the cooperative corporation regarding an owner's improvements to the unit.
REF: p. 466

207. B

A condop is a building that has both condominium and cooperative ownership.
REF: p. 469

208. A

Pet restrictions and repair obligations are disclosed in the condominium's bylaws. A letter of intent is an agreement to purchase a condominium. A CPS1 statement contains the Attorney General's regulations to advertise and market the condominium before the offering plan is approved.
REF: pp. 470-471

209. D

During the CPS1 phase, the Attorney General will not allow the condominium or cooperative developer to set a definite price for the units.
REF: p. 473

210. C
The mansion tax is statewide and applies to one-, two- and three-unit properties as well as condominiums and cooperatives that sell for $1 million or more.
REF: p. 478

Commercial and Investment Real Estate
211. B
Depreciation is a tax-deductible paper loss that allows investors to show less income for tax purposes.
REF: p. 521

212. C
The mortgage principal is never tax deductible.
REF: pp. 510-511

213. C
$15,000 x 12 = $180,000 ; $180,000 ÷ $500,000 = 36 percent
REF: p. 493

214. D
$850,000 x .012 = $102,000
REF: p. 495

215. B
Property owners generally charge for the rentable square footage including elevators and hallways, not the usable square footage.
REF: p. 497

216. D
The natural breakeven point describes when an investor will generate a positive return. Attornment refers to a transfer of a right usually in a lease. Expense stop is a type of lease payment arrangement.
REF: p. 498

217. D
A lease clause that states that future owners cannot terminate a lease if the owner fulfills his obligations is a nondisturbance clause. An escalation clause allows for increments in the lease payment. An estoppel clause confirms the lease terms. A subordination clause subordinates a lease to any mortgages on the property.
REF: p. 500

218. A
A type of lease escalation clause is the Porter's wage formula that allows lease increments according to the Porter's hourly wage. Estoppel, use, and subordination clauses are other types of lease clauses.
REF: p. 501

219. A
Generally, the more dollars the investor risks or puts up for an investment, the greater his return.
REF: p. 485

220. C
Leverage, or borrowed funds, describes the use of other people's money. The more leverage an investor has, the less of his own funds he needs to put into the investment.
REF: p. 486

Income Tax Issues in Real Estate

221. D

According to IRS rules, property taxes are deductible for a personal residence, a second home, and an inherited property. Real property taxes are deductible for commercial real estate as well.
REF: p. 510

222. C

By law, the long-term (12 or more months) capital gains tax is 15 percent for property owners in the 15 percent tax bracket and above.
REF: p. 511

223. D

Petro's misfortune is not tax deductible.
REF: p. 511

224. C

According to regulations for a 1031 exchange, a personal residence is not eligible for a tax-deferred exchange.
REF: p. 514

225. B

Appraisal fees, notary fees, and a mortgage preparation fee do not qualify for a tax deduction. Points, under certain conditions, are tax deductible.
REF: p. 519

226. A

The main housing credit agency in New York is the NYS Division of Housing and Community Renewal. HUD is a federal housing agency. FEMA is a federal agency that addresses various disasters. The NYS Division of Human Rights addresses civil rights issues.
REF: p. 521

227. D

According to IRS regulations, nonresidential property may be depreciated over 39 years.
REF: p. 522

228. B

The 59 1/2 rule allows first-time homebuyers to use IRA distributions to fund up to $10,000 of their new home cost without paying an early distribution penalty. Safe harbor laws apply to independent contractor status.
REF: p. 510

229. C

According IRS regulations for a tax-deferred exchange, a real estate exchangor has 45 days from the closing to contract for another (replacement) property.
REF: p. 516

230. D

In a tax-deferred exchange, any cash in the exchange is called the boot.
REF: p. 516

Mortgage Brokerage

231. A
The agency that registers mortgage brokers and mortgage bankers is the NYS Banking Department.
REF: p. 530

232. C
A NYS licensed real estate broker can use that experience to obtain a mortgage broker's license. A salesperson needs two years experience in the mortgage business.
REF: p. 530

233. A
A mortgage broker who represents a purchase in negotiating a mortgage loan has a fiduciary relationship with the client and is the client's agent.
REF: p. 531

234. C
A mortgage broker who represents the purchasers in negotiating a mortgage while also representing the sellers as a real estate broker in the same transaction is acting as a dual agent.
REF: p. 531

235. C
According to the banking law, a minimum line of credit to be register in New York as a mortgage banker is $1 million.
REF: p. 533

236. C
A lender's preapproval letter verifies the applicant's credit and employment history. This letter shows the capability of the purchaser to obtain a mortgage commitment although the letter is not a commitment. An appraisal is an estimate of value.
REF: p. 534

237. A
A request by a purchaser to reserve a certain loan interest rate for a specified time is called a rate lock. A commitment is a promise by a lender to make a mortgage loan. A rate cap is a limit on an interest rate.
REF: p. 535

238. D
Loan underwriting is the process in which the financial data and credit history for a prospective borrower is analyzed by the lender. Pre approval requires that a lender validate a borrower's credit and employment history. This evaluation precedes the underwriting process and is not as involved.
REF: p. 535

239. D
A lender's rebate is a form of payment to a mortgage broker for negotiating a loan from the lender.
REF: pp 536-537

240. C
A loan that does not meet the Federal Bank loan criteria for funding is called a nonconforming loan. A straight term loan is one that may have interest only payments in the early stages of the loan.
REF: p. 536

Property Management

241. C

According to New York law, if a property manager works for one owner, he does not need a license.
REF: p. 543

242. A

The management agreement, which is a contract between the owner and the manager, creates an agency relationship between the two. The proposal outlines what the property manager will do for the owner. A listing agreement is an agreement to market a property. A letter of intent is an agreement to purchase a property.
REF: p. 544

243. B

In managing a property, risk management has to do with the liability of the owner when the public enters a property. This risk is covered by property insurance.
REF: p. 545

244. D

If a building is 98 percent occupied, the property manager may feel justified in raising the rents. This is because the building is already generating a positive cash flow and there is less risk due to competition.
REF: p. 547

245. D

Property income and expenses for week-to-week operations are computed in an operating budget. Cash flow is the profit after income and expenses are deducted. Capital reserve is a budget for repairs and improvements to the property. The stabilized budget is an income and expense projection over a number of years.
REF: p. 550

246. A

$750 x 6 = $4,500 x 12 = $54,000; 7 x $1,050 = $7,350 x 12 = $88,200; $88,200 + $54,000 = $142,200 x 0.05 = $7,110; $142,200 - $7,110 = $135,090.
REF: p. 551

247. B

The property management report relates expense items to the operating budget for a certain period. The property management agreement is the terms for management of the property agreed to between the manager and the owner. The rent roll is the total annual rents for the property. The stabilized budget is a projection of income and expenses over time.
REF: p. 554

248. C

Lydia's assessment of items that may need repair is an example of preventative maintenance. Actually repairing an item when needed is corrective maintenance.
REF: p. 552

249.D

If a property manager works for one owner, no special license or education is required. BOMI and IREM designations are obtained from professional property management organizations if certain requirements are met.
REF: p. 543

250. D
Alexa, as fiduciary and upstanding citizen, most disclose to the owner, all monies received, and place
these monies into the property management account.
REF: p. 554

Answer Key for Practice Exams

Practice Exam 1

License Law and Regulations
1. B
The salesperson and broker license terms are for two years.
REF: p. 11

2. C
A salesperson may receive compensation only from his sponsoring broker.
REF: p. 23

3. B
It is unlawful for a salesperson or broker to draw legal documents.
REF: p. 27

Law of Agency including Independent Contractor

4. C
A dual agent cannot give the fiduciary duty of undivided loyalty.
REF: p. 54

5. C
A local board of REALTORS® cannot set a commission schedule.
REF: p. 47

6. C
Belinda, because of her relationship with her broker, is a subagent of the principal. The broker is the agent
of the principal.
REF: p. 50

7. B
In buyer agency, the buyer is the principal.
REF: p. 61

8. A
From the choices in the question, the only circumstance where the disclosure form is required is when the
listing agreement is signed.
REF: p. 65

9. C

When two real estate firms conspire to charge the same commission rate, they are guilty of illegal price fixing. An illegal group boycott occurs when one group or person is persuaded or coerced to not do business with another group or person. An illegal market allocation agreement occurs when competing companies agree to split a territory among them.
REF: p. 49

10. A

Designated agent are agents in the same brokerage firm where one agent represents the buyer and the other represents the seller. Designated agency is used when a dual agency situation arises. A broker's agent is hired by another agent to work for the client.
REF: p. 59

11. B

Although many properties listed for sale have material defects, the agent has a duty to disclose the defects to all interested parties.
REF: p. 45

12. D

There is no requirement that all agents be dual agents, represent the seller, or belong to the multiple listing service. However, all types of agents that work together to bring about the real estate transaction are cooperating agents.
REF: pp. 50-51

13. C

A real estate salesperson who is an independent contractor, under IRS rules, is one who is not paid according to hours worked but according to an independent contractor agreement between the agent and the broker.
REF: p. 79

14. C

Independent contractors are governed by the Federal IRS code and conforming New York State statutes.
REF: pp. 78-79

Legal Issues
Estates and Interests

15. B

Tenancy in common occurs when two or more people hold title to a property at the same time. Joint tenancy and tenants by the entirety (husband and wife) are ownerships attained with the unities of time, title, interest, and possession. Ownership in severalty implies sole ownership.
REF: p. 104

16. B

Riparian rights belong to an owner of property bordering a flowing body of water. Chattel refers to personal property. Subsurface rights are rights to property below the surface of the earth. The bundle of rights is all of the rights inherent in real property ownership.
REF: p. 97

17. B
Sales contracts and purchase offers are used in the sale of real property. Juan will most likely use a bill of sale.
REF: 96

Legal Issues
Liens and Easements

18. B
Real property taxes are involuntary because they are imposed by the taxing jurisdiction. They are specific to the real property.
REF: p. 110

19. C
A mechanic's lien is a claim by someone who has performed work on a property and has not been paid. A lis pendens is a notice that a lawsuit is pending.
REF: p. 111

20. A
Goldie's property allows the easement so it is the servient tenement. An encroachment is the intrusion of an object on another's property. A lien is a change against another's property.
REF: p. 113

Legal Issues
Deeds

21. C
A deed must have an acknowledgment to be recorded. Not all deeds have a metes and bounds description, hadendum clause, or covenant of warranty.
REF: p. 123

22. D
An executor's deed, guardian's deed, and sheriff's deed are all forms of judicial deeds. A Torren's certificate is a title recording document used in some states and in Suffolk County, New York.
REF: p.129

Legal Issues
Title Closing and Costs

23. A
The purchase money mortgage is a form of seller financing. The seller is giving a mortgage rather than receiving money so it is a debit to the seller.
REF: p. 146

24. D
Delinquent real property taxes generally must be paid before a closing can take place. Most often, the seller pays his back taxes before closing.
REF: p. 146

The Contract of Sale and Leases
Leases
25. A
Because the lease contract has been transferred to Jamie, an assignment has taken place. Under a sublease, the original tenant, Amy, would be responsible for the lease payments. Constructive eviction occurs when the tenant is forced to move out of a leased premise because of unlivable conditions. A holdover tenancy occurs when a tenant remains in a leased premise after lease expiration.
REF: p. 176

The Contract of Sale and Leases
Contracts
26. A
Nancy had to pay Tessie liquidated damages. Had there been specific performance, Nancy may have had to pay the purchase price of the property. Rescission is a withdrawal of the contract. Novation is the substitution of new contract for an old contract.
REF: p. 186

The Contract of Sale and Leases
Contract Preparation
27. C
In order for a real estate salesperson to prepare a fill-in-the-blanks contract of sale approved by the Board of Realtors, it must contain an attorney review clause.
REF: p. 206

Real Estate Finance
28. D
A balloon mortgage is a type of mortgage that is not fully amortized. A larger payment, called a balloon, is due at the end of the mortgage term. A graduated payment is a type of mortgage in which payment is lower in the early years and increase on a scheduled basis. A wraparound mortgage is a subordinate mortgage that includes the same principal obligation secured by a first mortgage against the same property. It is a type of seller financing.
REF: p. 255

29. B
Equity of redemption occurs when a borrower who has defaulted on his loan may be able to regain his property by paying the outstanding debt. A deficiency judgment is a charge by a lender to parties who default on their loan and when a foreclosure proceeding does not cover the full debt on the property. A deed in lieu of foreclosure is a document transferring a property to the lender to avoid foreclosure proceedings.
REF: p. 234

30. C
The acceleration clause allows the lender to declare the entire balance due if the borrower defaults. The prepayment penalty clause is a fine imposed by the lender if the mortgage is paid off before it is due. The granting clause is part of a deed. The defeasance clause gives the borrower the right to pay off the loan.
REF: p. 228

31. B
A blanket mortgage allows two or more parcel to be pledge as security of the loan. A package mortgage allows personal property, in addition to real property, to be pledged to secure payment of the mortgage loan. A bridge loan is a short-term loan. An installment contract allows title to pass to the borrower once the mortgage obligations are fulfilled.
REF: p. 238

32. C
FHA, the Federal Housing Authority, is an agency of HUD. Fannie Mae, Sonny Mae, and Freddie Mac are not affiliated with HUD.
REF: p. 24

Land Use Regulations
33. B
Article 9-A is the New York law that regulates the sale of unimproved lots across state lines. The Interstate Land Sales Full Disclosure Act is a similar federal law. The State Environmental Quality Review Act is a New York law regulating environmental issues when land is improved. The Uniform Fire Prevention and Building Code is a New York construction code.
REF: p. 265

34. D
Condemnation is the act of taking a property after eminent domain. Escheat occurs when the government takes property of the deceased if no heirs are found. Estoppel is generally a court order to stop an act. In rem is a type of legal proceeding against real property and not the individual's personal property.
REF: p. 266

35. C
Emma would need an area variance. A use variance is to use the property for a certain purpose. A nonconforming use is one that already existed before the zoning was changed. Illegal spot zoning occurs when property does not conform to the surroundings
REF: p. 277

Construction and Environmental Issues
36. A
Foundations are poured concrete or concrete block.
REF: p. 293

37. C
The soffit is the area under the roof extension. The fascia is a board that is perpendicular to the soffit. The third component of the roof overhang is the frieze board. This is a wooden framing member fastened directly under the soffit, against the top of the wall. Sheathing is a plywood material that covers the roof rafters.
REF: p. 297

38. D
In the sale of one- and two-family residential properties as well as condominiums and cooperatives in New York, the seller must present a signed smoke alarm and carbon monoxide detector affidavit at closing. There may be one affidavit for the presence of both the smoke alarm and carbon monoxide detector.
REF: p. 309

39. B
The New York law that requires preparation of an environmental impact statement on properties that a government body has the jurisdiction to review is the State Environmental Quality Review Act. The Superfund Amendment and CERCLA have to do with liability upon transfer of title. The Real Estate Settlement Procedures Act is a federal law applying to real estate closings.
REF: p. 323

40. B

Disclosure of knowledge of the existence of leadbased paint must be made in the sale or lease of pre-1978 target residential properties.
REF: p. 315

Valuation Process and Pricing Properties

41. D

Because both the comparative market analysis and the sales comparison approach compare properties that are similar to the subject, the CMA is most similar to the sales comparison approach. The income (capitalization) approach and cost approach are other appraisal approaches to value.
REF: p. 343

42. A

Evaluations do not necessarily produce an estimate of value, as does an appraisal or CMA. Value in use is not a land utilization study but defines the usefulness of a property to the owner.
REF: p. 341

43. B

A real estate agent must be able to adjust the listing price according to the market.
REF: p. 352

Human Rights and Fair Housing

44. C

Testers are volunteers who visit real estate firms and other businesses to assess equal treatment for all.
REF: p. 362

45. D

Real estate agents cannot violate human rights laws in taking listings or any other real estate activity.
REF: p. 362

46. C

Illegal blockbusting includes prompting homeowners to sell their properties due to the entry of certain persons of a particular race or religion into the neighborhood
REF: p. 374

47. A

The lender is guilty of illegal redlining; that is, denying or restricting loans in a certain area by a lending institution. Steering is a practice by real estate brokers that encourages culturally diverse people toward or away from certain areas. Blockbusting occurs when real estate salespeople tell homeowners that a member of a protected class is moving into their neighborhood causing them to panic and place their homes for sale. These activities are all violations of the Federal Fair Housing Act.
REF: p. 375

Real Estate Mathematics

48. B

$90,000 x .06 = $5,400
$5,400 x .60 = $3,240
REF: p. 388

49. D

$217,500 x.02 = $4,350
REF: p. 399

Municipal Agencies
50. C
The planning board would most likely have the task of mapping a large parcel of land that was granted to the city. The assessor's office values property for tax purposes. The zoning board of appeals hears variance requests. The architectural review board oversees building design.
REF: p. 407

51. D
Francesca will have to apply for a variance so she will need to go before the zoning board of appeals. But she probably also has to gain approval for the project from the architectural review board. It is possible that the board will not allow the project and then she will not need to apply for the variance. The conservation advisory council oversees environmental issues including wetlands.
REF: p. 408

Property Insurance
52. B
The missing $1,000 is the deductible that is paid by the insured toward the claim before he receives any policy benefits. Perils are events that cause damage. An umbrella policy is an excess liability policy, providing additional coverage above that offered by primary policies. An endorsement is a document attached to the policy that modifies or changes the original policy in some way
REF: p.428

53. B
The coverage that the Lee's have is for replacement cost. Replacement cost means that the insured is covered and reimbursed for the actual cost of replacing the damaged property. Actual cash value means that the insured is reimbursed for the replacement cost minus the physical depreciation of the lost or damaged property. An umbrella policy is an excess liability policy providing additional coverage above that offered by primary policies.
REF: 425

Taxes and Assessments
54. D
The map referred to in the question is a tax map. A plat is a property map such as a subdivision map. A blueprint is an architect's rendering of a structure. A survey is a detailed rendering of the physical boundaries, elevations, and other details of a property.
REF: 436

55. D
A taxing unit that levies real property taxes can be a city, town, or county.
REF: 438

56. C
Residential assessment ratios are used for board of assessments review grievances and small claims hearings. They are not used if there are less than five residential sales that year in the taxing unit. They are also not used for revaluation projects or determining tax exemptions.
REF: p. 439

Condominiums and Cooperatives
57. D
A cooperative shareholder receives a proprietary lease to the unit, not a deed.
REF: p. 460

58. B
The owner or developer of a condominium or cooperative is called the sponsor. A trustor transfers a trust fund or other account to a trustee.
REF: p. 471

59. B
The CPS1 statement contains the Attorney General rules for testing the market for a new condominium or cooperative development. The UCC-1 statement is filed with the county clerk when a condominium is transferred. The Civil Practice Rules and Procedure (CPLR) addresses legal procedures in New York. Section 443 of the Real Property law addresses agency disclosure.
REF: p. 473

Commercial and Investment Properties
60. D
The proforma statement reflects a potential change in income and expenses. The cash flow statement, operating statement, and statement of net worth are other types of financial statements.
REF: p. 491

61. B
$2,250 x 12 = $27,000; $27,000 ÷ 0.07 = $385,714 (rounded)
REF: p. 495

62. B
A process that calculates the value of an asset in the past, present and future is called the time value of money. Leverage is the use of other people's money. Debt service is the payment of principal and interest. Net operating income is property expenses deducted from gross income.
REF: p. 485

63. C
$750,000 ÷$1,000,000 = 75 percent
REF: p. 487

64. D
Land does not necessarily have less resale value than other types of investment property.
REF: p. 487

65. B
Income received on a property without deducting expenses is gross income. Once expenses are deducted, the remaining monies are net income. NOI stands for net operating income. The net operating income is the operating income minus operating expenses and debt service or the cash flow. Debt service is the annual amount to be paid to pay off or reduce a loan.
REF: p. 491

66. C
Once all expenses and debt service are paid, the monies remaining are called cash flow. A tax shelter is method of protecting income from taxation. Gross income is income received without subtracting expenses. The cash-on-cash return is a value measurement for a property that considers the equity in the property measured against the cash flow.
REF: p. 491

67. D

The cash-on-cash return considers the equity in the property against the cash flow. The capitalization rate is the annual return that an investor expects to receive. The rate of return is the percentage amount that an investor receives back on the investment.

REF: p. 493

68. D

Just as other types of investments, like the stock market, for example, profit is never guaranteed for any type of investment.

REF: p. 485

Income Tax Issues in Real Estate Transactions

69. D

There is no 39 percent federal tax bracket for income tax purposes. The highest tax bracket is 35 percent.

REF: p. 510

70. D

According to the IRS, mortgage interest and property taxes are all federal tax deductions for property ownership.

REF: pp. 510-511

71. D

Annie and Xavier do not have to pay a capital gains tax on the sale of their property. They have lived in their house for five years and the profit on the sale of $50,000 is less than their $500,000 married couple exemption.

REF: p. 512

Mortgage Brokerage

72. A

If an applicant for a mortgage broker's license also holds a real estate broker's license, he must submit a dual agency affidavit to the banking department. An estoppel certificate may be included in a commercial lease.

REF: p. 531

73. C

A real estate salesperson needs two years of experience in the mortgage brokerage business to apply for a mortgage broker license. A licensed real estate broker can use this license as the experience for the mortgage broker license.

REF: p. 530

Property Management

74. D

Advisors to property managers who focus on long-term financing planning rather than day-to-day operations of the property are asset managers.

REF: p. 553

75. A

A document submitted to the property owner outlining the commitment of the property manager once he is employed is the management agreement. The management proposal is submitted before the agreement and outlines what the property manager plans to do.

REF: p. 544

Practice Exam 2

License Law and Regulations

1. C

A person must be at least 20 years old to be licensed as a real estate broker in New York.
REF: p. 11

2. A

Attorneys who are admitted to practice in the New York courts are exempt from obtaining a license as long as they do not employ salespeople.
REF: p. 14

3. B

According to New York law, brokers must maintain a separate escrow account for client monies including deposits. The office operating account must be separate.
REF: p. 27

Law of Agency including Independent Contractor

4. D

An illegal net listing contract allows the broker to keep as a commission any money obtained from the sale above a sale price specified by the seller.
REF: p. 27

5. D

A broker's agent is one who is hired by a broker to assist the broker in selling or finding a property for the principal.
REF: p. 41

6. A

Under New York law, dual agency is permissible with disclosure and informed consent of buyer and seller.
REF: p. 53

7. D

With an exclusive agency arrangement, the broker is legally entitled to the commission if the exclusive broker or another broker effects sale of the property, but not if the owner sells the property without the assistance of any broker. An exclusive-right-to-sell agreement allows the broker to receive a commission no matter who sells the property. An open listing arrangement allows the property to be listed with a number of brokers who receive a commission only if they sell the property. An illegal net listing contract allows the broker to keep as a commission any money obtained from the sale above a sale price specified by the seller.
REF: 65

8. C

The first law to address antitrust violations was the Sherman Antitrust Act. The Clayton Antitrust Act is another antitrust law. The Real Estate Settlement Procedures Act addresses regulations having to do with real estate closings.
REF: p. 49

9. B
This example illustrates an illegal tie-in arrangement because as a condition of sale, the buyer must obtain financing from a specified company. An illegal group boycott occurs when one group or person is persuaded or coerced to not do business with another group or person. An illegal market allocation agreement occurs when competing companies agree to split a territory among them.
REF: p. 50

10. B
An agency relationship created by an oral or written agreement between a principal and agent is an express agency. Implied agency can be created through the acts of the parties. Dual agency occurs when one broker represents the buyer and seller in the same transaction. A power of attorney allows a person to legally manage the affairs of another.
REF: p. 46

11. B
Under an exclusive-right-to-sell contract, Martin owes a commission to Broker Gerald even though Martin sells the house himself. This is a possible breach of contract. Reformation permits a court to rewrite a contract perhaps in case of a typographical or other mistake. Injunction is a court order to stop an act. Assignment is the giving over of the contract to another.
REF: p. 65

12. D
The brokerage firm typically owns the listing contracts.
REF: p. 46

13. C
In the independent contract relationship, there are no deductions taken for income taxes. Paying income tax is the responsibility of the licensee.
REF: p. 79

14. A
Real estate licensees are classified as independent contractors under Section 3508 (a) (b) of the IRS Code. Article 12-A applies to the New York salesperson and broker license law. Section 443 of the New York Real Property Law applies to agency disclosure.
REF: p. 79

Legal Issues
Estates and Interests
15. C
The unities that make up a joint tenancy are the unities of time, title, interest, and possession. Partition is a court action to divide a property owned by tenants in common.
REF: p. 104

16. B
The most complete ownership is fee simple absolute. Fee simple defeasible estates have conditions for ownership. A fee simple defeasible ownership is recognized by the words "but if" in the transfer. A life estate is ownership for a person's life or another's life.
REF: p. 100

17. D

This question is an example of a life estate. A fee simple absolute estate is complete title to a property. A leasehold estate is not ownership but rental. A joint tenancy is a type of ownership with the right of survivorship.
REF: p. 101

Legal Issues
Liens and Easements

18. D

A judgment is an involuntary general lien because it is without the permission of the property holder and can apply to all of his property.
REF: p. 111

19. B

A lis pendens is a notice that a lawsuit is pending affecting title or possession of a property. An injunction is a court order to stop an act. A judgment is a lien against all property of the debtor. A mechanic's lien is a lien for unpaid labor or materials.
REF: p. 111

20. C

Lionel's property requires an easement by necessity because it is landlocked and Lionel cannot leave the property any other way. An easement by condemnation is created by eminent domain. A negative easement is an easement not to do something such as block a view. An encroachment is the intrusion of an object across a boundary line.
REF: p. 116

Legal Issues
Deeds

21. C

A type of deed used in bankruptcy proceedings and foreclosures is a referee's deed. A sheriff's deed, executor's deed, and guardian's deed are other types of judicial deeds.
REF: p. 129

22. B

In order to claim title by adverse possession in New York, the use must be open and notorious for 10 years.
REF: p. 131

Legal Issues
Title Closing and Costs

23. C

Discount points, the hiring of an attorney by the purchaser, and a purchase money mortgage are all common closing events. Outstanding liens would generally delay a closing because the title would not be clear.
REF: p. 147

24. A

On the closing statement, the earnest money deposit appears a buyer credit. Prepaid real property taxes, a prepaid insurance premium, and the sale of personal property are all seller credits.
REF: p. 146

The Contract of Sale and Leases
Leases
25. B
A periodic lease automatically renews itself at the end of the term unless notice is given.
A proprietary lease is given to cooperative unit owners along with shares of stock as evidence of their ownership share.
REF: p. 169

The Contract of Sale and Leases
Contracts
26. A
An option is a unilateral contract because only one party, the optionor, makes a promise. The option specifies a time limit in which the optionee can choose to purchase. It is not a contract to convey title.
REF: p. 198

The Contract of Sale and Leases
Contract Preparation
27. D
Contingency clauses, addenda, and riders are all possible additions to the contract. A codicil is an addition to a will.
REF: 130

Real Estate Finance
28. C
A HUD agency (Department of Housing and Urban Development) that purchases VA (Department of Veteran's Affairs) and FHA (Federal Housing Administration) mortgages on the secondary market is Ginnie Mae (Government National Mortgage Association). RHS is the Rural Housing Service that makes loans and grants to rural properties. SONYMA is the State of New York Mortgage Agency that loans money for target properties. FDIC (Federal Deposit Insurance Corporation) insures bank deposits.
REF: p. 246

29. B
A mortgage clause that allows a lender to declare the balance due if the borrower sells the property is the alienation clause. The prepayment penalty clause is a fine imposed by the lender if the mortgage is paid off before it is due. The granting clause is part of a deed. The defeasance clause gives the borrower the right to pay off the loan.
REF: p. 229

30. D
A mortgage that provides for paying the debt by monthly payment of principal and interest and in which the interest portion of the payments decreases as the principal portion increases is an amortized loan. A balloon mortgage does not fully retire the debt. An installment land contract calls for a transfer of title after all payments are made. A swing loan is a type of short-term loan.
REF: p. 236

31. B
Regulation Z of the Truth-in-Lending Act addresses the accurate advertising of credit terms. The Real Estate Settlement Procedures Act addresses disclosure of closing costs. The Community Reinvestment Act encourages lenders to meet the credit needs of communities. The Anti-Predatory Lending Law is a New York law that places many restrictions on high-cost (subprime) loans that are first or junior mortgages.
REF: p. 247

32. A

An adjustable rate mortgage rate floats based on a standard index as opposed to a fixed rate that stays the same throughout the mortgage term. A straight term mortgage allows interest only payments for a specified time.
REF: p. 237

Land Use Regulations

33. B

In New York, variance requests are brought to the zoning board of appeals.
REF: p. 276-277

34. C

The boundaries and physical dimensions of a property are shown in a survey. A feasibility study determines a project's usefulness and projected success in the community. A plat is a subdivision map.
REF: p. 133

35. C

Parks and forests are classified as public open space. Institutional properties include hospitals and schools.
REF: p. 270

Construction and Environment

36. C

UFFI (urea formaldehyde foam insulation) is a type of spray-inside-the-wall insulation that is not longer allowed. This is because it contained irritating and unhealthful levels of formaldehyde. Loose fill, rigid, and batt are other types of insulation.
REF: p. 321

37. B

The amount of electrical current flowing though a wire is the amperage. Voltage is the force or push of the current. Milligauss is measurement of electromagnetic field strength.
REF: p. 305

38. B

The New York Energy Code mandates minimum R-factors for insulation. The Real Property Law addresses real estate license law and other property issues. The Emergency Tenant Protection Act governs rent control and rent regulations. The Sanitary Code is overseen by the NYS Health Department and addresses health and sanitation issues.
REF: p. 299

39. C

Senior citizen housing is generally exempt from disclosure under the Residential Lead-Based Hazard Reduction Act. The Act is aimed at children who might eat lead from paint chips and dirt.
REF: p. 315

40. A

One of the most prevalent concerns for underground storage tank is leakage caused over time by erosion, wear, and tear of the tank material.
REF: p. 324

Valuation Process and Pricing Properties

41. C
The aim of an accurate CMA is to find properties in as close proximity as possible to the subject property.
REF: p. 343

42. B
Surveyors and appraisers fees in relation property development are indirect costs. Hard or direct costs are costs for labor and materials. Impact fees are made to the municipality by a developer for infrastructure and other requirements.
REF: p. 342

43. A
An arm's length transaction means that the parties are not related as relatives or business associates.
REF: p. 342

Human Rights and Fair Housing

44. D
In New York, in the sale of a single-family home, there are no exemptions in the New York Human Rights Law whether or not Hattie uses the services of a real estate broker. She also cannot discriminate against a person's race in any real property sale as this violates the federal Civil Rights Act of 1868 where there are no exemptions for racial discrimination.
REF: p. 371

45. C
The fine for a first offense in violation of the Federal Fair Housing Act can be up to $10,000.
REF: p. 373

46. B
According to the New York Human Rights law, brokerage offices must display the HUD fair housing poster.
REF: p. 363

47. C
Both New York and federal law address discrimination based on familial state, disability, and sex. The Federal law, however, has fewer protected classes than New York.
REF: p. 370

Real Estate Mathematics

48. D
$3 \times \$8,000 = \$24,000$; $\$9,000 \times 4 = \$36,000$; $\$36,000 - \$24,000 = \$12,000 = 50$ percent
REF: p. 496

49. C
$150 \times 500 = 75,000$ sq ft; $75,000 \div 43,560$ sq ft/acres $= 1.72$ acres
1.72 acres x $5,000 = $8,600 acreage basis; $20 x 500 = $10,000 front foot basis
REF: p. 392

Municipal Agencies

50. B

The building department oversees compliance with the building code, inspects properties during and after construction, and issues building permits. Government agencies in New York cannot require property owners to restore or rehabilitate a historic structure.
REF: pp. 410-411

51. A

The conservation advisory council accepts grants made to the municipality for lands under its jurisdiction such as wetlands. The planning board oversees land use issues. The architectural review board oversees building design. The building department oversees the building code.
REF: p. 410

Property Insurance

52. B

Perils are events that cause damage and are included on the insurance policy. Some perils are excluded from basic policies but may be added to the policy or obtained in a separate policy (i.e. flood insurance.) Lenders require homeowner's insurance to obtain a mortgage, an endorsement is an attachment to the insurance policy, and an insurance policy is a legal contract.
REF: p. 422

53. D

Usually, additional property coverage, such as a storage shed, is covered at 10 percent of the residence limit. Therefore, the residence was insured for $200,000.
REF: p. 426

Taxes and Assessments

54. B

The level of assessment is the percentage of market value at which properties are assessed. $300,000 × .75 = $225,000.
REF: p. 439

55. C

The purpose of a special assessment is to collect payment for a share of improvements made to the area. A judicial review of a tax protest in the New York Supreme Court is called a tax certiorari proceeding. Reassessments can be performed on properties when improvements are made, and on a regular prescribed basis. The tax levy is the amount that a municipality must raise to meet budgetary requirements by taxing real property.
REF: p. 444

56. A

An in rem legal proceeding is a legal action brought against the real property and not against an individual and his personal property. An injunction is a court order to stop a specific action. A judicial review of a tax protest in the New York Supreme Court is called a tax certiorari proceeding. A reformation is a court order that permits the parties to rewrite a contract when a mistake such as a clerical error is made.
REF: p. 452

Condominiums and Cooperatives
57. B
In a cooperative, the board of directors must approve a prospective buyer.
REF: p. 466

58. C
In a cooperative, the cooperative corporation owns the common areas.
REF: p. 460

59. D
The alteration agreement is a contract between the shareholder and the cooperative to make structural changes to the unit. A letter of intent is an agreement to purchase a condominium that may or may not be binding. House rules govern daily behavior in the cooperative. Subscription agreements are the contracts that the sponsor possesses to purchase shares of stock in the cooperative units. These agreements are included in the offering plan to the attorney general.
REF: p. 464

Commercial and Investment Properties
60. D
$20,000 x 12 =$240,000; $240,000 ÷ $600,000 = 40 percent
REF: p. 493

61. A
The profit from income producing properties, less income taxes is the after cash tax flow. The before cash tax flow is profit before income taxes. Debt service is the payment of principal and interest. Debt is what the investor owes. Equity is the investor's interest in the property. The debt-to-equity ratio describes the percentage of the capital that is invested.
REF: p. 493

62. B
$10,000 + $2,000 = $12,000; $12,000 x 0.35 = $4,200
REF: p. 493

63. D
A paper income loss on investment property is called a tax shelter. Gross income is income received without deducting operating expenses. Debt service is the payment of principal and interest. Leverage is the use of other people's money.
REF: p. 493

64. D
$650,000 ÷ 0.12 = $5,416,667 (rounded)
REF: p. 495

65. A
Property owners lease commercial space according to the rentable square footage that is the entire space. The usable square footage does not include elevators and hallways, for example.
REF: p. 497

66. B
The loss factor is the area that is part of the rented space that is not specifically usable to the tenant.
REF: p. 497

67. A
A loft is a type of commercial space that is not generally divided into rooms.
REF: p. 498

68. B
Unlike many residential leases, a commercial lease is generally customized. This is because most spaces are unique and there are different tenant needs for each. A periodic lease automatically renews itself for another period at the end of each period unless one party gives notice to the other at the prescribed time.
REF: p. 498

Income Tax Issues in Real Estate Transactions
69. B
The basis is the cost of the property. The adjusted basis includes other costs such as the fire that devalued the property.
REF: p. 513

70. B
A limited partner does not materially participate in the managing and operation of the investment. Therefore, under the IRS code, Hurry's income from the investment is classified as a passive activity. Active income includes salaries or income from a business in which the taxpayer materially participates. Portfolio income is interest, annuities, dividends, royalties, and profits from the sale of portfolio assets.
REF: p. 513

71. C
In a tax-deferred exchange, the individual who accepts the funds from the sale and handles the contract is called the qualified intermediary (QI).
REF: p. 516

Mortgage Brokerage
72. D
The pre-application disclosure and fee agreement is used by mortgage brokers to make certain disclosures regarding the mortgage fee and other matters. The agency disclosure form is used to disclose whom the real estate agent represents in the sale of rental of one-to-four unit residential properties. A pre approval letter is a document from a lender stating that a purchaser is pre approved for a loan. A letter of intent is an agreement to purchase a property such as condominium.
REF: p. 531

73. D
A mortgage banker is licensed by the NYS Banking Department.
REF: p. 533

Property Management
74. D
There are various fee arrangements between a property manager and owner. One of them is a base fee and a percentage of the rents collected.
REF: p. 545

75. D
Because they perform a variety of duties, property managers are general agents. A special agent generally performs one duty such as marketing the real estate. Because of their role as agents, a fiduciary relationship, a position of trust, exists between the manager and the owner.
REF: p. 543

Notes

Notes

Notes

Notes

Notes

Notes

Notes

Notes

Notes

Notes